Wo/Man, Work IT Out!

Remodeling Work Culture through Your Success

Wo/Man, Work IT Out!

Discover Your True Self
&
Realize Your Full Potential

By

Tejal Rathod

Copyright © 2024 Tejal Rathod

All rights reserved.

ISBN: 9798320217239

This publication is designed to provide accurate and authoritative information in regard to the subject matter covered. The persons, personnel, entities, and events portrayed in this book are real. For privacy reasons, some names, roles, locations, and dates may have been changed. By works of this book, the author does not intend to draw any undue influence from or harm any real persons, living or dead, or any entity or establishment in any way or form. While the publisher and author have used their best efforts in preparing this book, they make no representations or warranties with respect to the accuracy or completeness of the contents of this book and specifically disclaim any implied warranties of merchantability or fitness for a particular purpose. No warranty may be created or extended by sales representatives or written sales materials. The advice and strategies contained herein may not be suitable for your situation. You should consult with a professional when appropriate. Neither the publisher nor the author shall be liable for any damage, monetary or non-monetary, loss of profit, or any other commercial damages, including but not limited to special, incidental, consequential, personal, or other damages.

No part of this book may be reproduced, or stored in a retrieval system, or transmitted in any form or by any means, electronic, mechanical, photocopying, recording, or otherwise, without the prior written permission of the publisher or author. For permission requests, contact authortejalrathod@gmail.com.

Cover Design, Layout, and Illustrations: Tejal Rathod
Cover Photograph: Canva Images
Author Photograph: Reel-On Chemistry
Publisher: Tejal Rathod
01 Edition. Publication 2024.

Tejal Rathod
www.elementsdcoach.com
Wo/Man, Work IT Out!
Discover Your True Self & Realize Your Full Potential.
Remodeling Work Culture through Your Success.

To all those who dare to have dreams!
To all those dreams that breathe & live!
To all those dreams that are impossible until they are possible!
And
To all those endeavors, transforming your success with meaning & happiness!

Contents

Preface	*1*
PART I. Introduction	*13*
Chapters from My Life	*14*
What brings me here with you?	*21*
Will you consider?	*23*
PART II. Living the Reality!	*27*
1. Motivation	*29*
2. Mindset	*41*
3. Accountability	*53*
4. Collaboration, Teamwork & Allyship	*61*
PART III. Living the Dream!	*75*
5. Having it All!	*77*
6. The Skills Game	*81*
7. Values for Character	*99*
8. Work-Life Balance	*119*
9. Culture of Diversity	*127*

PART IV. Being the Dream! — 143

10. Not just Intellect — 145
11. Uncovering the Truth! — 163
12. Power of Health — 181

PART V. The Bridge — 191

PART VI. The Plan! — 195

13. The Master Model — 197
14. Work IT Out - Framework — 211

PART VII. What's Next? — 223

Your Journey — 225

About Author — *233*
Afterword — *237*
Acknowledgments — *241*
References — *243*

Wo/Man, Work IT Out!

Preface

What's this about?

Wo/Man, Work IT Out! redefines success for individuals & working professionals through personal growth and creating a value-based work culture in any organization. Knowing what success means to anyone is primal, knowing oneself is vital, knowing one's dreams is fundamental, and finding meaning & happiness in success is crucial. Accessing those dreams need not be far from one's reach, and converging personal & professional life need not be difficult. This book addresses the fundamental need of individuals to bring clarity to their dreams and explains the process of achieving them. It covers key success disciplines, models, guiding principles, processes, and framework to integrate the essential aspects of outlining a work-life strategy. Ultimately, building up a Work IT Out - master plan that can help every individual & working professional to achieve their dreams and emerge as a *Star* while bridging their personal & professional aspirations. The book is a reference for individual professionals and organizations to ponder the most important questions & stereotypes to attain personal & collective growth. This book gives quintessentially timeless, practical, actionable professional insights and learnings based on the author's diverse first-hand work experiences. Any professional can relate to discussed subjects and work dynamics that are interleaved with authentic and candid professional scenes from the author's two-decades-long journey as a corporate woman.

Following the book's well-rounded and progressive working protocols allows anybody to chart their tailored path to success, from living the realities to achieving their dreams. All while having fun at it!

Is this for you?

In today's fast-paced, growth-centric, and high-stress working environments, this book provides a practical guide for individuals and organizations to achieve their visions successfully. Essentially, this book is meant for readers who are either aspiring or already established working professionals. The subject matter discussed here is relevant to the world audience: Men & Women alike, a Leader in Business, HR, Marketing, Legal, Sales, or any other discipline, a mid-level Manager, or an Organization at any stage of their professional journey.

If you are a self-starter or a follower, like to lead or to get things done, prefer to plan or to take action, this book can be used as a self-mentoring tool by every working professional who likes to take charge of their lives to see sustained and long-term success. Readers looking forward to integrating their personal and professional priorities through self-discovery and using their full potential will benefit the most from this book. Timeless, practical, and actionable insights covered through this book ensure that anyone can transform their success with meaning & happiness.

What can you expect?

What remains a dream can be achieved beyond just professional life's realities. Those dreams are attainable, and there is a path to achieving them. The disciplines, aspects, and principles discussed throughout this book are meant for progressive and incremental change. Long-term success is guaranteed by defining and pursuing one's tailored definition and meaning of success. In a world where generalized professional advice, strategies, and guidance are increasingly becoming mundane & irrelevant, this book provides access to the essential disciplines, models, processes, framework, and micro-strategies to customize your path and achieve your dreams through your personal growth—helping you to build a blueprint of work-life happiness.

If you are looking for a mentor, look no further! This book is a self-mentoring working guide to chart a customized plan for achieving your personal and professional goals. With anticipated challenges, new perspectives, techniques, and guidance, this book gives you novel approaches to solving the most critical underlying obstacles to reaching your goals. There is objective guidance & ideas that everyone can apply to look for the best possible outcomes.

While working through an outline of your life goals, this book systematically integrates key aspects of the professional and personal arena. With every chapter, there are practice time exercises to work along. These present ideas and hypotheses targeted towards individuals, teams, leaders, and organizations to undertake. These exercises are nothing but micro-strategies for curating a progressive future for yourself and the corporate world at large, which can help you take action to develop various vital disciplines required to succeed. It provides practical micro-strategies on how to keep personal growth at the center of any work-life endeavor to build a solid foundation for your long-term happiness. The simple and easy-to-practice micro-actions you'll design through this book can compound their positive effect on your life over time. Helping you to swiftly navigate different career stages by cultivating an attitude of never settling for less, a win-win work culture, promoting a value-based mindset, and asking the right questions to discover yourself & seek answers to. At the end of the book, you'll have a concrete work-life strategy tailored to your needs that contains tangible, individualized insights about your dreams and prioritized goals. Along with micro-strategies to take action on and an aggregated Work IT Out - master plan to make your growth journey guaranteed satisfying and successful.

What is stopping you from becoming a *Star*?

- Why would anyone care for personal growth?
- Why would anyone care to look into the future?
- Why would anyone care to integrate personal and professional goals?
- What does success mean to me?

- How do I define my success?
- Why would anyone plan their success & happiness?
- Why would anyone dare & care to follow their dreams?

While receiving a steady, predictable paycheck that guarantees continued support to their lives, professionals often neglect to answer any of these questions. This way of working through life could work well for a short period but not for sustained, long-term success. Life is unpredictable instead of being as steady and permanent as it may seem. Some factors affect our lives more than we think they do. For instance, changing geo-political environment, economic policies, financial outlooks, wars between nations, newly developed treaties between regions or countries, worldwide pandemic, changing generational cultures & their respective demands, changing governments in power, environmental changes, technological advancements, etc. All these and more can cause indirect or sometimes even direct life changes. Amongst such volatility in external circumstances that are out of our control, our lives can change at any time, now or in the future. Being prepared, adaptive, and flexible is required to deal with such situations. Additionally, with every passing year, businesses are becoming more demanding of their workforce to deliver high business value. Inducing the stress that can be manageable only if we are vigilant about how our lives span through time and where they go. How can one come out of survival mode to thrive? How can one keep up with their vision through good or turbulent times?

A few of you may argue that embracing uncertainty and being prepared for the same could be a function of having the foresight to predict future events. We know having such foresight is difficult to achieve, with a greater degree of certainty & assurance that they won't affect our personal & professional lives adversely. We hope to figure out a solution to such external uncertainties someday. But today, we can be prepared to handle uncertainties or adversities in our personal & professional lives through deliberately and systematically planning for them. Another of you may also prefer to leave your progress, majorly relying on chance, thinking no amount of planning can stop what is inevitable from happening. This approach works for those who do not even dare to have dreams for their lives. Everyone can take a chance to lead their lives or be led by it. Both approaches are acceptable. But here we are speaking to professionals who believe in endeavors and want to make a difference in others' & their lives while sustaining through the volatility of the new-age corporate world.

Rather than being submissively passive about what works in reality, i.e., a steady paycheck & a few work opportunities, you can benefit from being proactive, thinking ahead, and being intentional about charting your success plan for achieving dreams and becoming a *Star*. Allowing you to learn from successfully working models, processes, frameworks, and micro-strategies. A Work IT Out - master plan that makes you think longer term, make progress with the changing world, and, as a result, make your dreams come true. Knowing what to be prepared for and how to achieve it could be an excellent start to pursuing your respective goals.

- What is good for others at large? Is it good for me too?
- If not, how do I know the WHYs, WHATs, and HOWs of something that matters for my success?
- How often do I wish to know what I don't know?
- How often do I want to take action on something I know?
- How often do I want to continue the course despite all odds?
- How often do I want to challenge my complacency and status quo?
- How often do I want to dare and have a dream to achieve?

To answer these questions, in retrospect, many of us often pacify ourselves and continue living our realities, saying,

- 'I wish I knew it before!'
- 'I wish I had done it before!'
- 'I wish I had been out there earlier!'

How often do you tell this to yourself?
Now is the time to make these reasons of the past!

Beginning to address various challenges faced on a day-to-day basis, such as having a continuous source of motivation, not being able to keep up with the struggles of increasing expectations and delivering better than the best, changing priorities, keeping up with the work-life balance, cultivating the mindset of a marathoner, building & sustaining endless energy sources, keeping up with ever-changing demands of up-to-date skills, and not finding the right supportive environment, opportunities, or guides. At the bottom of it all, most importantly, overcoming self-doubt, filling the gaps of self-awareness, dealing with your innate fears & insecurities, and exercising self-control. All of these can be worked with simple, easy-to-use, incremental steps that lead to not just living your professional realities but going beyond realities towards achieving your seemingly impossible dreams. Additionally, suppose you have ever encountered yourself stuck believing some of the thoughts (mentioned below). In that case, you'll find an overarching useful approach mentioned throughout this book to address them collectively. With the help of explained growth disciplines and practices to develop them, you can ensure that your endeavors become more fulfilling and wholehearted.

1. Dreams are not for me.
2. Only perfect individuals get promoted.
3. Career growth is all about compensation, title, and position.
4. Career growth is only important in the early stage of your professional life.
5. A high salary is the ultimate measure of success.
6. Only numbers matter in business!
7. Work-life balance is not possible!
8. Belonging is all about trendy perks and fun benefits offered.
9. Behaviors have no bearing on my promotion!
10. Functional skills are enough for success!
11. It's impossible to keep up with the ever-changing demands of up-to-date skills.
12. I don't seem to find the right supportive environment, opportunities, or guides.
13. Work culture does not affect a company's bottom line.
14. Work culture is problematic to change.

15. Hard work always leads to success.
16. Everyone can do it, have it all, but me! I don't have it in me! I am not good enough for it.
17. Work-life balance cannot be my reality! Burnouts are real, and I can't do much about them. Everyone is going through it.
18. I'll burn out if I have the mindset of a marathoner! I lack in building & sustaining endless energy.
19. Because everyone says it, I am not good enough for the job!
20. Only a few of those who have in them can stay motivated.
21. No one can keep up with the struggles of changing & increasing expectations.
22. I am not cut out to deliver better than the best!
23. Changing priorities and demands of work are impossible to address.
24. It's not my problem to deal with.
25. My life will be like a million others!
26. Happiness and satisfaction only come from work/job.
27. There is no reason to care about the company's vision & mission in my work position!
28. Being a working woman is a curse!
29. Women are losing their ambition!
30. Workplace flexibility is a woman's thing.
31. Microaggressions and unpleasant behaviors don't matter!
32. Corporate culture must grow organically.
33. Company-wide, the work culture should remain similar.
34. Work culture is driven by company values & employee satisfaction surveys.
35. Great work culture is controlled from top to bottom by executives & human resources.
36. Inter-generational gaps are problematic for a company's future.
37. Work culture is just another gimmick.
38. The company's work culture can be quickly improved.
39. High-paying companies have a bad work culture.
40. Work-life balance is not essential for an incredible work culture.

Why this one?

When so much information is already available, why is there a need for another book?

Well, because the information in itself has no value until you figure out what your context is, i.e., defining your success, purpose, vision, dreams, mission, needs, priorities, etc. Additionally, it's essential to know what strategies work for your context and how to apply those strategies effectively to clock your goals.

This book sets a different tone through

- Providing an exploratory playground to discover & grow yourself.
- Understanding what is most important based on your needs and stage in life.
- Giving Work IT Out - disciplines, models, framework, processes, micro-strategies, master plan, and tools to define and customize your context.
- Combining personal and professional journeys.
- Putting forth different strategies for individuals, teams, leaders, and organizations to cultivate a healthy and supportive work culture.
- Well-functioning guidance that is time-tested, practical, and future-proof.
- Accessing guidance in one place as a self-mentoring working guide.

Like every other professional, at some point in the author's career, she has also had doubts about her current and future growth. Her questions were endless:

- What does success mean to me?
- Where does my future lie?
- Does the future hold any space for achieving my dreams?
- Am I living my dream or someone else's?
- Where am I being led to?
- Am I doing the right thing?
- What am I contributing to?

- What am I receiving?
- Are my contributions worthwhile?

A lot of collective experience surrounded her, but when she had numerous such questions, there was negligible guidance that she could find useful in the context that worked for HER! She found that the answers to most of the questions lie within one's approach toward personal growth and how to identify & function optimally within one's circle of influence. This book speaks about the unspoken stereotypes and realities through the author's encounters. With that knowledge accessible easily, you no longer need to say to yourself, 'Only if I knew this earlier' or 'I knew it all the way, but all I needed was permission to go ahead.'. It covers insights from first-hand experiences that the author has lived through twenty years of working with diverse organizations, businesses, geolocations, roles, and teams. These experiences are unique to one professional but relatable to many. Situations when she doubted that success was out of reach. But after taking the help of various self-help books, devising & working through various research-backed strategies herself and on teams she worked with, learning from those experiments, and improvising along the way, all of it resulted in outcomes that made things possible for her. And so it can for you too! Amidst daily, never-ending uncertain times, staying on course and taking on experiences & opportunities as they came by, helped her stay in the arena rather than just wondering or being trapped in negative, hopeless thinking.

While it's true to some degree that every problem at the outset may seem very generic, with a set of high-level solutions to follow and solve, this thinking works until it stops working! We all reach that stage when generalized guidance and taking things as they come no longer work. Guidance on how one can make it individualized to their context is the need of the hour; one size no longer fits all! Perspectives and strategies presented in this book are worth pondering over to know yourself better. They apply to anyone and can be practiced by anyone on their own. Proving that the new keys to your success are not out there but within you, know how to identify them! Systematically curating what works for you, being intentional about it, and making it roll into an action plan is what this self-paced working guide will help you achieve. Yes, you have hit the jackpot with the simple, easy-to-use, and practical working practices laid out here; they are timeless and future-ready.

You may believe that, in this journey, there might be many factors out of your reach to change, which is true to a certain degree. But your personal growth remains within your bounds of control. Your success is paramount to your growth & to the growth of the organization you work with, but most importantly, to the work culture we all aspire to breathe in daily. We live in a world where everyone is interconnected and interrelated by many means. Knowing how to leverage our shared common interests is one of the keys to success & happiness. A journey of personal growth makes this happen! The beauty of interconnectedness multiplies the good around us, the growth that comes from within and spreads around us.

How to read this book?

Wo/Man, Work IT Out! is a book highlighting the needs of a successfully functioning corporate world. Although lived through the experiences encountered by a corporate woman, the book is meant for working professionals agnostic of their gender, industry, expertise, level of role or title or position, and country of operation. Every corporate professional can benefit from the outlined guidance, including organizations that want to think beyond business-as-usual (BAU) practices and truly bring value to their customers by caring for their workforce. At the same time, think outside the box and challenge the status quo by leaping beyond the mindset of matching *what other organizations are doing*.

Work IT Out - disciplines, models, framework, processes & micro-strategies discussed in this book help individuals and organizations to remodel their personal growth & work culture. Personal and professional life need not be mutually exclusive anymore. They can be harmoniously integrated with utmost clarity on one's needs, entailing a long, meaningful life. How does one achieve that? By following the framework discussed in this book. Explore, define, and converge your purpose, vision, mission, goals, and micro-strategies into your dreams.

Working through the book (not just reading through) is recommended as a self-mentoring working guide. Therefore, following the sequence of chapters, one at a time, as the book progresses is the recommended course for the best outcomes. Additionally, going back to chapters multiple times as and when required can help distill acquired understanding. Remember that this book is your playground, and it comes alive when you work through every question mentioned to identify your realistic context, i.e., your success, aspirations, situation, environment, vision, mission, needs, goals, priorities, etc., and by following the *Work IT Out - Framework* process. Work through the practice time exercises mentioned after each chapter by pausing and reflecting on the subject matter discussed in that chapter. To log outcomes, download the *Worksheet: Work IT Out - Framework*; refer to the *Resources* section of *Chapter - Your Journey*. These exercises apply to every professional regardless of role, title, position, and level.

Additionally, practice time exercises will lead you through a journey from reality to dreams in three main stages (or goals), building your context gradually as you work through the book.

1. Living the Reality!
2. Living the Dream!
3. Being the Dream!

In principle, each stage is explained through the lens of essential aspects and personal growth disciplines that you can develop to make progress toward achieving overall meaning, success, and happiness in your pursuits. Where each growth discipline of a stage talks about micro-strategies and actions required to figure out *WHAT* does matter live that stage (goal); only these chapters can be independently read if you must.

Further, integrating three stages (goals) with the help of two primary constructs:

1. *Work IT Out - Master Model*
   To overlay micro-strategies with guiding principles & a priority model, making a high-level blueprint to figure out *WHY* it matters to access dream success.

2. *Work IT Out - Framework & Process*
   To align strategies and master models into a final framework that brings it all together, answering, *HOW* does one approach accessing their dream success?

In case you have surpassed the subject matter & practices discussed in this book, my heartiest congratulations on your progress! Let's engage further. For details, refer to the *Resources* section of *Chapter - Your Journey*.

Hope you have a great time exploring your dreams and achieving them!

PART I

Introduction

*'It's not the strongest of the species that survives nor the most intelligent.
It is the one that is the most adaptable to change.'*

- Charles Darwin, English Naturalist, Geologist, and Biologist

Chapters from My Life

Coming from a humble family based in Mumbai - India, I grew up in a positive traditional household of micro-business owners. I was surrounded by old, wise souls who always encouraged me to learn from new and diverse experiences as I was growing up. There was a greater emphasis on pursuing education and doing the right thing. While heavily focusing on academic pursuits, I also enjoyed cultivating interests in extracurriculars like arts, music, light sports, and travel. I managed to get good grades and stood amongst the top 5% in the class then. In India, state board exams are milestones to crossover and pursue graduate education. Before higher education, there were two important legs to cross: 10th and 12th grade. After doing fairly well in my early school years, my biggest challenge awaited me after grade 10th. The challenge was the language! Having been schooled in a vernacular medium, I now set out to pursue the science stream education in a language I needed to be more accustomed to. Now onwards, any education would be in English. The expectations were to be just as good, if not more, as I did so far, despite my thinking and studying languages being different. So far, my exposure to English has been the bare minimum, through watching some random television shows that made no sense to me, with a fundamental elementary-level proficiency.

From the outside, this seemed a typical problem to many. But it was the toughest I have handled so far. Struggling to convert every word of a sentence into a foreign language was a mountainous task. My mind could not comprehend many things, often making me feel confused, rejected, and disappointed. From the world around me came the gut-crunching feelings of shaming, mocking, bullying, neglect, and disrespect, all of which became part of my everyday life experience. On top of that, I absorbed & internalized this negativity within myself as if I deserved it. Making ends meet was like learning new words while making sense of a whole sentence. Cultivating basic understanding was a far-fetched thought; what to speak of learning from it. In the competitive environment I was exposed to, it rarely worked to seek support. Everyone wanted to get through their education with flying colors to ensure a better future. What came to help was the mindset that I learned from my tuition teacher in the 10th grade. She taught me an approach to pursue two completely different sets of learning paths simultaneously and effectively; in my case, it was learning a new language and a science subject matter. This struggle continued for the next six years until my graduation, as during those years, I incrementally pursued the practice of observation and deliberately developing new vocabulary.

In hindsight, what was happening within me was the power of incremental change. I was holding on to my grit to make it work and let it not be the reason for my failure. The power of keeping hope alive and continuing to work at it, the attitude of being more observant, being sensitive to the surrounding environment, cultivating integrity to keep me truthful about my capabilities, doing right by others because I had experienced what it feels like to be brushed out, and being ready to learn as much as I can; this continued till many years into my professional work life. This intrinsic motivation to prove myself worthy of everything that came towards me was always present. While I was grateful for the grit I held on to, I resented the feelings of fear and failure many times during the day, weeks, months, and years altogether. While harboring self-doubt and questioning my worth, my determination to do the right thing helped. Graduating from one of the city's premier engineering colleges of my time was a feather in my cap through these times. It was my ticket to achieving my dreams and being self-sufficient.

Through the next twenty years in the corporate world, my attempts at looking for the right job, working through the personal & professional responsibilities at hand, carving my space in the industry, and contributing the value I add to customers, everything was all-consuming, challenging, yet satisfying. With the realities of life as they hit, there were many changes in terms of changing the city & country that I lived in, roles & higher education that I pursued, and keeping up with growing expectations of doing better than the best every passing year. As I became tenured within the industry,

I met with more responsibilities, expectations, standards, and valued impact to deliver. I also battled through some of the myths mentioned earlier myself, like

- Focusing on a steady income versus pursuing new avenues.
- Making decisions to change roles versus pursue specialized education.
- Continuing with my current organization versus exploring new opportunities elsewhere.
- Managing personal & professional lives together equally.
- Managing biases at the workplace.
- Continuing to do the right thing no matter how difficult it gets.
- Working hard to improve myself at every opportunity inside out.
- Working through numerous fears and insecurities of finding stability.
- Dealing with my emotional & physical well-being.
- Dealing with the restlessness of doing & being my best at everything, every time.
- Working through a high-performing environment, etc.

Raising this game was not an easy task as I dealt with a lot of resistance internally from harboring self-doubt & disappointments of not being good enough, succumbing to external peer pressure, getting stuck in unnecessarily imposed competition, my elevated expectations from myself, exposure to dysfunctional work cultures, and struggles of inconsistent health. I only knew better once I learned from my experiences, and they were a mixed bag, some good and some not so pleasant. Eventually, I recalled them as good events throughout my career, as they helped me build my character as I lived through them. These seemingly challenging times taught me what success means to me, how to dream & aim bigger, and how to pursue self-reflection as my go-to tool to keep me connected to reality. It helped me build a work-life strategy that integrated my personal and professional goals and that can work as a model for any working professional.

At some point in my career, everything was going well but not good enough to alleviate my itch to build a venture focusing on creating a quality impact for customers through technological adoption. The thought of going on my own was daunting because of my high expectations of myself to work it out. But the hardest to deal with was my internal voice of succumbing to a golden cage, things that I had to let go of, i.e., a good salary, growing role, aspirational opportunities, etc., available right at the peak of my career, the stability that I had always desired. On the other side of this stability, I was facing my fears or insecurities of an Entrepreneurship world in which I had no direct experience working and minimum knowledge of potential struggles waiting for me to deal with. It was a high-stakes decision for me. After much deliberation & weighing my options carefully, I took a leap of faith and went with making my new dream come true. My new adventure worked until it did not! With my changing aspirations & personal priorities, I pivoted my career back into technology consulting. I noted that, as time passed, my dreams shaped and evolved into something bigger, allowing me to expand my capabilities more than I thought. These capabilities helped me reach the masses, give more, attribute scale, and create valued societal contributions. After a few years of working with one of the Big 5 technology companies, a dilemma again hit. However, I liked the value technology brought into the world. I knew that I had outgrown and reached the peak of what I could directly contribute to the world of technology. Being part of it, I deeply felt gratitude for the opportunities I have received to see my personal & professional growth thus far. But now, I had outgrown my needs and capabilities in that arena. This time around, I was battling the question of health & purpose! I found that leading others to their success through learning from my past was more gratifying. As I speak, I live that purpose daily, bringing meaning, honor, and respect to every life through my coaching practice. So that anyone can empower, transform, and evolve themselves, as it happened for me. Looking back at my journey, these experiences taught me about

- Discovering myself & my surroundings at the deepest levels to cultivate awareness that matters.
- Integrating personal and professional life courses seamlessly. Health is an integral part of it.

- Managing myself through self-reflection, observation, retrospectives, and experimentation.
- Knowing what matters to me and defining my life vision accordingly.
- What to focus on for long-term, meaningful success.
- What affects a healthy and harmonious culture in the workplace?
- Dealing effectively with different personas.
- Delivering impactful quality results for customers & organizations across various sizes, geography & industry.
- Managing the insecurities of others, yet continue to keep the focus on productivity.
- Continuing to build interpersonal relationships within cross-functional business groups and teams.
- Shaping my professional values and challenging the status quo when necessary.
- Working to build my credibility and individual worth.
- Innovatively expanding my knowledge and experience base by contributing to new things apart from my day job at work.
- Cultivating professionalism while having fun at work.
- Understanding the intent, efforts, and outcomes from all sides involved in a given situation.

It helped me grow into a professional with a value-based growth mindset rather than settling for anything and accepting the status quo without questioning. These experiences were rich in themselves but more challenging than they seem. They required immense personal integrity, authenticity, objective curiosity, conducive ambition, hard & smart work, courage & bravery, and a professional mindset. I didn't have it all at once when I began, but they were intentionally, incrementally, and consciously developed through years of practice.

In my journey, what did success mean? How did I make it work for many years being engaged in diverse environments? What did personal growth mean? How did it all culminate into being meaningful? These are the answers I found in discovering my true self and realizing my full potential. I.e., having self-knowledge & self-awareness of my position in life, in other words, knowing my changing life context well enough at a given time. What mattered was a change in the mindset, *'What am I harmoniously giving and creating in the world? How many lives am I impacting positively, directly or indirectly.'* Rather than thinking about *'What did I receive at the end?'.*

This path has helped me fulfill my dreams and given me many insights, like

- Finding my true self through self-discovery.
- Living in the moment while being mindful of purpose or end goal.
- Change of mindset & values for long-term, meaningful success.
- Self-sufficiency over self-reliance or independence.
- Never settle for less. The win/win approach makes it work.
- Redefining my success while functioning in the corporation.
- Made to think of strategies & overcome distractions, fears, or insecurities of being shamed, tagged, and locked out of growth.
- Constraints & lack of resources breed innovation and new ways of doing things.
- Discernment about what your circle of influence is.
- Cultivated habits for life to expand my perspectives by self-reflecting and embracing life events gracefully.
- Focusing on the endeavor and not just the outcomes.
- Doing things better, not just for results but for the sake of doing it.
- Total health is a matter of collectively focusing on the wellness of body, mind, and spirit.
- Knowing the difference between means and end.
- Empowering thyself with knowledge & wisdom.
- Transforming yourself with hope and seemingly impossible change.
- Evolving thyself with change in consciousness.

Time and again, as I found others telling me I couldn't do it, I heard I could. I took it as an opportunity, and I worked it out. Through all of my situations, experiments, and learnings came a set of growth disciplines and models that worked for me and many others with whom I worked and mentored. Models centered around defining what kind of success works for one considering all sides involved, what is realistically possible, how personal growth can help them attain it, how a holistic approach focusing on body - mind - soul can make goals more meaningful, and how a deliberate work-life strategy can act as a starter tool to plan dreams and get into action. Learnings composed through this book capture all of these experiences, growth disciplines, models, framework, processes, micro-strategies, and tools that cater to world readers. That is, individuals who set out to go through a similar future of achieving their seemingly impossible dreams but with a different trajectory that works for them. Knowing that our destination remains the same while our approach may differ. Knowing that our questions remain the same while our paths to achieve success may vary. What matters is that you seek to make your mark in the world through your contribution, primarily through your professional and personal life alongside each other, to attain long-term success & happiness alike.

What brings me here with you?

These experiences and learnings took from me an open mind, willingness, determination, time, effort, dedication, attention, and commitment. But I reached where I intended to; I started and worked my way up in the professional world. I began as someone trying to find her ground while others were already flying jet planes. I started as any other software graduate and worked her way to her dreams. If this is possible for me, it is for you, too!

My journey entailed working across many software engineering disciplines with customers of different industry domains, geographies, and various-sized organizations & teams, as well as working with the world's most recognized workplaces in the technology space. This rich and diverse experience has led me to adjust and readjust my path to personal growth to accommodate the environment and demands of customer outcomes. With time, I converted my challenges into opportunities by deeply going through good, bad, or ugly experiences and developing successful working strategies to solve the problems at hand. It makes me believe that the possibilities are immense for your dreams to succeed if you dare to achieve them the right way!

For most of my tenure in the information technology industry, there was hardly any concept of having formal mentors available. In comparison, only privileged executives could access coaches. This was when, in numerous self-help books, I found the mentors & coaches that I needed. It slowly opened my perspectives and expanded my outlook on success, which is not far out there but right next to you: Within you! I always wanted to develop practical, proven guidance that can help replicate customized success for anyone and that is easy to follow by experimenting with myself, my surroundings, & the teams I worked with. And here it is, made available for your consumption at once.

Looking back, I have lived through wonderful, successful years in the corporate world by having an enriching time cultivating myself into a world-class professional. As an Entrepreneur today, I better understand and consider the journeys of all sides involved to make businesses work well, i.e., employees, leaders in various functions, managers, customers, cross-functional teams, vendors, organizations, etc. My expanded worldview & perspectives through continued education in Executive Management, Psychology, and Health & Nutrition have helped me actively engage in communities related to mentoring, coaching, skills development, value-based character development, and total health, catering to audiences at the executive level and in their early-mid career levels. This journey was not what I dreamed of on day one at my first job; the dreams progressively changed. Had I had early access to some of the learnings (listed through this book), then my pace of growth could have been much faster, clarity of my next steps would have been much better, and I could have possibly achieved my dreams much more meaningfully. Having said that, I am glad to have gone through these experiences precisely the way they transpired in my journey. They kept nudging me enough for many years to keep evolving, and they still do. As they say, there is no better teacher than adversity.

I have this opportunity to pass this knowledge to you now, hoping it will be greatly useful in any form. Wishing that you find your dreams and the will to pursue them, bringing the positive change our personal & professional world needs to see.

Starting from humble beginnings, if I can, then you can too!

Will you consider?

If you ever dreamt of having personal & professional success accessible, dreaming big, achieving those dreams well, making a positive impact in the community, country, or world, and leaving a legacy that everyone joyfully welcomes in the future by touching human lives deeply, then keep reading this book.

- Will you say 'Yes' to yourself?
- Will you consider gaining new ideas and perspectives?
- Will you work through the insights covered in this book?
- Will you consider gifting yourself the benefits of the following aspects?

Journey
Live through this journey towards your dreams in three stages (or goals):
1. Living the Reality!
2. Living the Dream!
3. Being the Dream!

This book discusses the growth disciplines entailed in each stage and how developing them can transform your day-to-day experiences into success. Success is realized by discovering your true self, thereby realizing your full potential.

Personal Growth
For most of you, if you have read books or specifically any self-help books, you know by now that for every problem, there is a book that exists in the world. For every changing problem, there is a need for unique & relevant

perspectives and solutions to apply. We are always making ends meet with the ever-changing nature of things, which is also valid for constantly changing work demands. So, our natural thinking is that every solution has to change with changing problems, and one needs to keep up with it to stay relevant. But what if you were told that there is a permanent model and an outline that can be used no matter what industry you belong to and the organization you are part of? Too good to be true? No, It's possible; the key is to keep your personal growth at the center of your workings. When most of us focus only on complying with getting outcomes as expected, we often lose the unique DNA or perspectives we bring to the table as our unique selling proposition (USP), i.e., our best selves to our respective organizations. Putting our efforts into growing ourselves inside out is the real meaning of getting our act together!

Personal Mentor

It is often found that reading different self-help books contributes immensely to the practicality of living life compared to any formal systematic education one can receive, be it undergraduate, graduate, or executive education. With this book, you can chart your pace, space, and reflections on the discussed subjects as effectively as you are your mentor. And make it work for you in real life!

Practical Guide

This book covers learning and self-guided practices that emerged from real-world challenges, obstacles, mistakes, and learnings. Practices that are simple to experiment with and are tested for success. Guidance, models, framework, and strategies discussed here can help self-mentor until you find a formal mentor, coach, or guide. Yes, this guide is nowhere a replacement for personal guidance, as we all need formal mentors and/or coaches occasionally for different purposes! A working guide is provided to work through, develop an exploratory mindset to answer questions, and curate a unique set of goals to work towards; both are subjective and customizable based on your needs.

Real-world Challenges

You can gain a new perspective from relatable real-world stories addressing small things that are often neglected but make a huge difference and matter the most. Knowing better is essential for long-term sustained success. Knowing how to incrementally work on resolving challenges and what matters beyond skills & outcomes can keep you paving the path to success, personally or professionally.

Individuals, Teams, Leaders, Organizations

Here is your one place to learn how to outline your success through personal growth in the professional arena. The laid-out guidance is for any working professional to adopt agnostic of their gender, role, title, or position within their organization or team. Specific practices listed here are for individuals, teams, leaders, and organizations to experiment.

Everything in one place

Subject matters discussed here give you a one-stop shop covering the journey of pursuing your personal & professional life dreams: knowledge that is accessible to everyone, which is the most essential, and available before they need it. By the end of the book, you would have made great use of your time introspecting over self-discovery questions and exploring provided practices, with the bonus of a developed work-life strategy & plan to execute your defined criteria for success. You will be ready & equipped to begin your path from living the reality to achieving your dreams.

PART II

Living the Reality!

> *'Either you deal with what is reality, or you can be sure that the reality is going to deal with you.'*
>
> *- Alex Haley, American Author*

Our lives give us abundant realizations of our reality. Whether it's getting ready for the day, staying motivated to work through it, getting people in the family to set their days, daily setting up of meals, planning the rest of the day, attending to chores, gearing up for the challenges at work, commuting to work, attend to late night work calls, attend to emergency emails, or responding to urgent messages of work, etc. We are all consumed in this reality day in & day out.
Do we even realize whether we are flowing with life? Or Is life carrying us somewhere, based on someone's command?

We seldom have time to stop and think, pause and reflect, gain a new perspective, or plan to gather what we want our realities to be. If you are a dreamer and carry any desires, you want a life full of possibilities that excite you & bring the most profound meaning, honor, and respect. But for many of us, reality is just about wanting to achieve happiness. Have you paused for a while and asked yourself,

- What does being happy mean to me?
- What does having a meaningful life mean to me?
- What does living with dignity, i.e., honor or respect, mean to me?
- Do I have a choice to carry a dream?
- Is what I go through the reality I want?

Answers to these questions can be different for everyone. But few realities do not change when it comes to work. Be it our most essential priorities and responsibilities at work. Or that next promotion. Or the subsequent conferences to prepare or attend. Or those meetings to plan for. Or planning & attending those customer/client visits. They all make it into our everyday reality at work. In the beginning, managing all of them together may feel overwhelming. But as we go through them, day after day, it becomes our everyday routine. To function at our optimum and achieve this run-of-the-mill state of life, we need some growth disciplines cultivated in our professional lives. For a corporate professional, these growth disciplines matter whether one pays attention to them, as they form the foundation for living our realities.

A reality exists beyond just living our responsibilities for which we are accountable. That reality is being hopeful while we are at it. The first stage in achieving success is *Living the Reality!* The foundation that empowers individuals to make their dreams come true.

What does it take for one to live such a reality?

CHAPTER 1

Motivation

'The best motivation always comes from within.'

- Michael Johnson, American Martial Artist

Scene One

In the summer, I moved to an urban city in India, working for a new organization. While I was excited for the new & upcoming, with a sense of mystery about what's in store for me, I was also perplexed out of nowhere. What if the new environment isn't conducive and imposes more challenges to work through? Will I be able to adjust to this newness? Will I be able to surpass obstacles on the way? My brain was not ready to accept more new things. After moving to a new city and adjusting to the new ways of going around, I was resisting more struggles. With a bit of hope and resistance, I landed on the first day to resume my work in an IT Park. At the outset, everything looked put together: clean, structured, well-planned, welcoming, futuristic, progressive, and professional. Little did I know that my actual feelings of being exposed to a herd of people daily going in and out of the IT Park would not be so positive. After all, with work being challenging, I thought these not-so-positive feelings would soon pass by and consume me with new responsibilities. Nothing of that sort happened! I found myself saying daily, 'My life is going to be like a million others!'. And I am not sure why that thought popped up daily in my head. I was bewildered, thinking, how everyone around me is just OK and going about their way through this mechanical & mundane life course? As if this is the best and the only thing everyone ought to experience. The only answer I could find was that this was not helping me move toward my happiness. I figured it was the issue of Motivation!

Scene Two

I was excited to attend my first-ever software technology conference (tech conference). As I entered the conference hall, packed with thousands of enthusiastic professionals as I was, I could find many familiar faces and new ones around me. Seeing so many workshops for hands-on learning, booths of various software products, and live demonstrations of working prototypes made from new-age technology was fantastic; Innovation that can change people's lives by making them more convenient and accessible! I was excited and deeply enjoying the experience like a kid in a candy store! Individuals who were present contributed so much to the energy of the overall event. It was exhilarating to be part of it! But the best experience came when I sat through a keynote speech by the CEO of a financial services company and how they are changing the Banking Industry through digital transformation using software products. This was when smartphones were beginning to be introduced to the world. Hearing the speech left me with a one-of-a-kind 50 minutes of my life. The speaker was inspiring, collected, objective, engaging, and highly impactful. I wondered what I could take back from his message, from him, and the collective experience those 50 minutes gave me. A kick to move in a direction that I had never ventured in. What I took back was the Motivation!

Scene Three

I was battling through an internal dialogue within myself. In the end, a conversation had to give me a black-or-white answer. A dialogue that centered around my fears of losing everything I had and venturing into something new by myself. After a familiarity of working in the corporate world for nearly 14 years, I was battling to know if I was ready to start my journey of being an Entrepreneur. A venture I had dreamed of building in business strategy consulting & technology solutions for B2B customers. Through these years in the IT industry, I could hardly manage time to read anything beyond purely technical subjects. It was about time when I picked up on reading non-fiction books, and to my surprise, I was a new loyal customer of the self-help books. It was the right time as I had never had a formal professional mentor. This reading gave me a reason to explore the avenue of reading more. It opened up a portal to welcome a series of deeply engaging authors, who soon became my new mentors and coaches in life. I was happy to pick up many books, but the one that stood out was *How Google Works* by Eric Schmidt and Jonathan Rosenberg. The excitement was because I always wanted to work for one of the MAANG (Meta, Amazon, Apple, Netflix, Google) like product companies, to experience the work culture that delivers world-class products & services to their customers. Reading the book would only add to my knowledge of how the Big 5 operates in the technology world. The book was the most satisfying journey, despite I was just sitting and reading. Why did that happen? I thought to myself it was because the subject matter resonated with me. Every word had perspectives I considered a dream come true and never knew existed elsewhere. Unique perspectives practiced as active, practical principles, a way of working for real! Those days of reading left me with a deep sense of excitement. It was Motivation!

All these scenes from different parts of my professional journey motivated me for different reasons. Through different methods, for different periods, for different durations, and a different depth of impact, they made on my psyche. Which was the best, according to me? The correct question is, which was the right motivation for me? And what was right about that motivation that worked for me? Identifying what is right for anyone can be contextual, i.e., it may or may not work for others. But in these scenes, something did have a common effect on many: a common pattern experienced by many. It was how motivation worked in different ways. From professionals who were present in that conference arena in scene one to somebody like me around the world who read the book in scene three, everyone experienced motivation. It can be through an uplifting or lacking phenomenon, often called a motivation gap.

But can we identify if anyone is suffering from a motivation gap? Can it be defined that a lack of motivation causes any energy slump? Yes, it's possible. If one is self-observant and has enough capacity to reflect and access the impact their surroundings, environment, and people have in their lives.

- If you succumb to distractions easily while knowing your priorities well, you are up for a motivation gap.
- If you are increasingly finding reasons to settle for less, then it might be caused by a motivation gap.
- If you do not have any direction, the motivation gap has kicked in.
- If you seldom feel bored through tasks, then there could be a motivation gap at play.

Many such instances can show us some red flags to identify if we are experiencing a lack of motivation. But what's the big deal about even having a constant stream of motivation? Why should it matter in the first place when you see many people who are just going about their day as if they are intrinsically motivated and not concerned about identifying if they lack motivation for something? Then why should it matter to you?

It should matter, and it matters to every living being internally. It's difficult to identify those who struggle to get motivated in their lives just by looking at people from the outside. Externally, everything may seem to be going in a straight line, as linear as possible. But reality is far from it. We, as human beings, are hardwired to be creatures of hope. And motivation lies on the bedrock of desire & hope. Many call it 'having a purpose,' but there is a subtle difference between them. Many would know their purpose but are not motivated to go and do something about it. Yes, motivation is that urge to take a leap of faith and finally act on THE THING! Every single time, every single day, every single moment. For most of us, this process is on auto-pilot or subconscious, so we do not realize it works behind the scenes. For instance, we get up in the morning and do our chores, e.g., brushing our teeth. It's a chore that most of us are programmed to perform. Do we need motivation to do that? For the most part, it looks like No, but we already have static motivation built and hard-wired within us not to feel the need to struggle for more. It just happens.

Another reason why motivation is required or necessary is that we all have desires, wishes, goals, and dreams to achieve in life to find our object of happiness. For that, the inertia required to keep us moving is nothing but motivation. Some may say that having material desires or desiring power, status, and ranking would motivate us enough to live. But it's far from the truth and reality. A rational individual soon understands the transient nature of such motivations. They are tied to our basic needs, which we will discuss in *Chapter - Uncovering the Truth!* The question remains of what one requires to practice and have a continuous, abundant source of motivation all the time. Before we get into that, let's understand different types of motivations.

From the scenes we saw earlier, I struggled to understand how three different situations provided me with such different experiences of motivation.

- The first scene provided me with an experience of 'I have to do it,' or 'I need to do it.' or 'Everyone does it, so I am also doing it.'.
- The second provided me with an experience of looking forward to my current pursuits in a more positive way. The internal inertia got triggered and stayed with me for a few months till I had faint memories of the event and the keynote speech; some new information caught my mind's attention.
- The third one had the most lasting impact on my motivation, and it still does (that's why it's getting a mention here). It lasted for years.

How is it that each experience left me with minimal to lasting impact on my motivation levels? If you assess closely, the driver and the method of motivation are very different in each situation I experienced.

- Through scene one, I felt force-fitted in an environment that made the least impact on my fundamental identity and motivation; on the contrary, it ended up creating a motivation gap.
- Through scene two, I got influenced by somebody else's vision, ideas, perspectives, words, and persona, which gave me a little more sustainable energy to stay put with my pursuits; it motivated me for a couple of months.
- And scene three resonated with my deepest beliefs and life values. The impact of it on my motivation still lasts longer than the other two experiences.

Does that mean that our beliefs drive our motivations for the most part? Yes and No. We shall discuss beliefs further in *Chapter - Values for Character*. For now, on the subject of motivation, the question for any layman remains: How do I keep my motivation high with the least effort? i.e., continuous supply of motivation every single day. It's possible to achieve this daily, but as humans, we must accept that we don't need active motivation to function second to second, as some of our internal programming will take over our functions and run in autopilot mode anyway. One need not disturb that flow either by being hyper-vigilant and feeling unsettled about deliberately creating a constant flow of motivation every second. Motivations can be driven by two primary methods: Extrinsic and Intrinsic. Both have pros-cons, but they are interchangeably used to drive the desired outcome, as per the need and circumstances we are put into.

Some methods to practice Extrinsic Motivation include

1. Being intentional about prioritizing your desires or day-to-day activities.
2. Being intentional about planning them out as a rough sketch of tasks one wants to achieve daily, weekly, and monthly. But also

Motivation

knowing to avoid getting lost in planning and only spending optimal time curating the list.
3. Setting goals that are possible but difficult to achieve.
4. Breaking your goals into smaller, simpler, and achievable tasks (things to do).
5. Choosing to do one thing at a time to retain the focus while staying in sight of an end goal or desired outcome.
6. Taking additional responsibility will require you to function more inertly.
7. Choosing to inspire yourself through content from speakers you admire, following an interesting subject matter, and any relevant workshops that can keep your right brain engaged enough to keep up your left brain doing the required logical work.
8. Build a community for driving contributions to things you love doing and find individuals with common interests. As giving has more power than one can realize, that created goodwill can chase you, opening up more opportunities for yourself & others. Creating a community of like-minded individuals working on like-minded goals & objectives gives one space for balancing concerns of their self-interest and the interests of others harmoniously. That proves to be a great motivation for many, without having to suffer burnout themselves caused by giving or falling short on the supply of motivation.

Some methods to practice Intrinsic Motivation include

1. Every day, we need a burst of motivation 'to trigger the energy within us' to continue doing the work in autopilot mode. Attaining that intentional reinforcement of what you say to yourself and controlling your internal dialogue subtly on a positive note can work like magic. What do I mean by that? It simply needs you to write your daily script you speak to yourself about. A script of life you want, the attitude you want, the state of mind you want, acting as if it's already part of you. Such scripting can be the most powerful tool one can use, only if you choose to believe that it

works. Most of us would discard such simple solutions without giving them a go only because they sound ridiculously simple. The fact is, most problems would require simple solutions. Simple things are hard to persist and sustain because of their inherent quality of being mundane and instigating boredom. But once persevered through the practice, one can see their intrinsic motivation at an all-time high. Yes, it has now become a part of the autopilot programming you always wanted.

2. Choose to work for an organization whose vision, mission, and values you believe in. Yes, choosing a role with which your skills are aligned is the first criterion to work with any organization, but the next could be an organization's values. Why? Because that has the most intrinsic impact on your motivations. Humans connect with things, objects, people, and environments that are more likely to find commonality in our beliefs, values, or things we value. Our shared visions, interests, or beliefs triumph over any authority put through force or compliance-driven work culture. Chances are that a company whose beliefs and values you resonate with will be able to provide you with the right environment to function day in and day out. Then, there would not be any need for constant motivational speeches or dialogues from leaders or managers to keep you on the course. They would most likely be busy recruiting and keeping a team that aligns closely (not perfectly) with those values & beliefs.

3. Another tangible thing you can work on is to increase your capacity to self-reflect and observe your surroundings objectively. Your depth of self-awareness can inhibit and elevate your personal & professional growth. As humans are built to resist things that are good for us, asserting ourselves towards change is not easy. Our minds constantly seek to remain in the domain of familiarity, which can hinder our progress. By being observant of your surroundings and cultivating self-awareness, you can understand the reality when you are deliberately resisting change and accordingly can take

intentional action on a task.

4. Manage the laziness syndrome. Laziness syndrome is about experiencing extreme laziness, lack of willingness to do anything or severe lack of motivation. Laziness is neither absolutely good nor absolutely bad. Accepting that occasional laziness is needed to stay in creative thinking. One can practice self-compassion over self-criticism and provide the internal support an individual seeks to come out of laziness. Practicing mindfulness regularly when not doing anything can help overcome persistent laziness. Be mindful of the difference between laziness and bodily fatigue; the latter is an experience of a possible health issue.

Motivation is nothing less than oxygen to live through the challenging realities of our lives. It gives us the necessary vigor and nudge required to continue living our daily realities. Motivation is easier to come by when things are going well. The key is to exercise regulation when significant struggles are met. If we accept self-motivation as a solution, then most of our lives can turn to having quality, creating value, and flowing harmoniously with life at ease. We steadily become more comfortable being uncomfortable with things draining our most essential source of energy & inspiration.

Practice time. Let's get to it!

- Extrinsic Motivation Method
    1. Write three goals you want to set.
    2. Split them into day, week, month, and year categories.
    3. Assign a priority to them based on the desired outcome you wish to achieve.
    4. Break them down into achievable tasks.
    5. Follow through them by tracking them at the end of the day. This activity should take only 2 minutes.

- Intrinsic Motivation Method
    1. Write a script of motivational speech for yourself and act as if it's happened. Look for a free mobile app in the *Resources* section of *Chapter - Your Journey*.
    2. Record the script in your voice using any recording app. Preferably keep it where you can access it easily daily, like on your mobile.
    3. Make listening to it a part of your daily routine. Write the time of the day and the number of times you'll remind yourself of it. This should take no more than 3 to 5 minutes.
    4. Listen to it for at least 30 to 60 days without a break.

1. Individuals
    a. Make a list of Intrinsic & Extrinsic Motivation Methods covered in this chapter that you would like to practice.
    b. Plan each practice to incorporate into your daily routine.
    c. Act on it as per plan.

2. Teams
    a. Conduct the exercise of Intrinsic Motivation Method (mentioned above), considering the team's goals & perspective in mind. E.g., team motivation.
    b. Play it at the start of the day or the beginning of scheduled team meetings.

- c. Keep at it for at least 30 to 60 days without a break.

3. Organization
    a. Adopt the Intrinsic Motivation Method (mentioned above) by popping up a scripted video as a mandatory auto-run admin program on every employee's computer.
    b. Offer adequate training or workshops to cultivate Extrinsic Motivation Methods.

CHAPTER 2

Mindset

'Do the best you can until you know better. Then when you know better, do better.'

- Maya Angelou, American Writer, Poet, and Civil Rights Activist

During the first two years of my graduation in the Computer Science discipline of Engineering, the curriculum was less than interesting. These subjects were not relevant to my choice of specialization. The subject matter was complex for me to grasp, understand, and live the life it deserved. I struggled due to my thinking language being vernacular and my study language being English. It naturally slowed me down compared to my peers. I had to continue putting extra effort into understanding words and sentences. Make them coherent in my mind, and then try to understand the context, followed by the concept. I needed to understand more than just the concepts; I had to devise a method to remember them. This was a very complex process for a nineteen-year-old woman. I needed more than smaller lab experiments for many subjects to understand their relevance in practice. Along with the language barrier, understanding the application of the subject in practical life & future career was a matter of concern. Adding to my struggles, this further proved to be demotivating and fearful.

My objective was to get through those subjects and stand with reasonable grades. With no confidante to share my real challenges, I adopted a different approach to studying. One month before the exam, during the preparatory leaves, I kept my head down in books and filled my brain with all the information I could from academic textbooks and notes I had prepared from lectures during the term. After trying various study groups, I realized I would not receive any support from folks who have not lived through my challenges. They could hardly notice them, so expecting any understanding was a far-fetched thought. They all meant to help, but it didn't help. Rather, being with them during study preparations kept my morals further down than I would want them to be. My expectation of myself to do well in academics, as I had done so far, led me to focus on achieving good grades. I didn't know any better way then. Learning a subject deeply and with all my heart & interest was a dream in this brutal reality I was living with. Learning, in a true sense, was at bay for me. My vernacular background led me to spend a lot of energy and time procrastinating because of the fear of failure. Not knowing I've already reached a point of failure.

The leftover positive self-belief in my capabilities helped me sail through this period. And a few years down the line, I finally found myself! I felt fulfilled, successful, happy, and creating meaning for others. Finally, I had crossed over the language barrier! That was when I started learning new products and technologies that weren't taught during my academic years, but I had to learn them on the job. This was to support my work deliverables and achieve customer goals effectively. I felt a renewed sense of confidence. Working with my teammates was fun & inspiring, and I welcomed the constructive feedback from my peers. Everyone was learning something new, which was practically used and contributing from their past experiences. We spent nights at hand getting together and working through many experiments. When they worked, it was an amazing joy that we experienced. And when they failed, it didn't pinch much as we had solid support from our leaders and managers. They trusted each one of us to figure it out eventually and keep up the work deliverables within the time committed to the customer. They showed us that keeping trust in the process, our abilities, and forming support don't have to be just lip service, but they can be practiced. They gave us an environment where mistakes were embraced as part of the learning process. Seeking constructive feedback, proactively correcting our mistakes, and not giving up on our efforts mattered more. They chose to acknowledge us all equally without making any petty distinction based on our position, roles, smarts, intellects, experiences, backgrounds, or individual capacities. We had challenges internally, but they seemed small enough to care about or brood over compared to the kind of support we received. We were consumed by the more rewarding exploration work waiting for us every day.

I truly felt that I had evolved in that period! I found a new deep understanding of myself that my challenging pace of learning (caused by the language barrier) did not limit me. In the past, that became a big reason for slowing me down or constantly worrying about standing worthy and being truly accepted by others. This time around, all that didn't matter. That was the point when I fully accepted myself as I was. I uncovered a crucial revelation about myself that would have otherwise gone unnoticed. I truly learned from my experience that

- Struggles are good. Openly accepting them and actively pursuing them can help one lighten the burden of fear within themselves. A sense of achievement that one gets simply following the attitude of 'I can do it by trying it' works wonders.
- Learning anything can be a journey; one doesn't need to figure out everything all at once.
- Accepting feedback, keeping healthy room for making mistakes, and staying persistent in making efforts to correct mistakes make a lot of difference to enjoying the process of learning.
- Reflecting on past experiences can help one learn much about themselves and shape their learning into knowledge.
- One can always know a lot about any subject. But accepting that 'I know nothing' can help one stay in a perpetual state of learning.
- Learning is the most essential aspect of living our realities well enough.

A few years later, I came across an academic researcher and psychologist named Carol Dweck through her book *Mindset: The New Psychology of Success,* which resonated with my personal experiences. Her research on the other side of the continent about how name tags of smarts, intelligent, super achievers, or any kind of awe-based praise was limiting individuals to stay within the bounds of something called Fixed Mindset. Reading this, I now found a proper definition to match my experience! I felt relieved as I was not alone in this journey, facing challenges that only I knew. I understood that what I experienced until my graduating years was primarily a fixed mindset and how my circumstantial opportunities during my early employment years turned it into cultivating a Growth Mindset.

These experiences proved that everyone has the capability to learn one or more things with varying degrees of impact. The pace, outcome, and ranking do little to our sense of fulfillment when we learn and grow. These are subjective factors, and that's the beauty of it. Learning through fundamental aspects is the key rather than by some means of achieving socially accepted outcomes. Taking on unnecessary burdens and pressures of living up to those social models of rankings or heightened expectations greatly influences our mindset concerning our target end. That means it affects our state of mind if we work and keep expecting rewards over joy, keep eying for acceptance from others, and live by a certain image over experiencing the flow of deep fulfillment & joyful moments that any learning can offer us. Regarding mindset, why should learning matter to us as much as we care about acceptance from others? Because we are hard-wired as humans to evolve through our developed abilities, comprehending new experiences & perspectives through intellect, logic, and intelligence. It can draw us closer to our purpose or newfound interest to contribute productively and progressively to the world. It can keep our minds engaged for a long time with a sense of satisfaction and ease while we live our daily realities. It has powerful effects on our motivations and our overall health in general.

Retrospectively, a few things helped in my journey of cultivating a Growth Mindset that can help others equally.

1. Going through a fixed mindset cycle during the academic years, I received support from maintaining good self-belief & acceptance of my capabilities. This attitude helped me flourish through that period and sustain it positively. On the other hand, while working within a team on the job, managers and leaders stood by us with genuine, empathetic support without piling on undue pressures of blame, shame, or guilt. It was this assurance that worked that someone had our backs even if we occasionally failed at experiments. This support mattered. In both cases, be it self-support or external support, accepting that failures are integral to the process of learning and growing helps maintain continuity.

2. One counts on collaborative peer groups for individual growth. When that happens, willingly helping others becomes a natural thing to reciprocate. Such collaborative communities can help professionals practice mutual respect, build trust, explore creativity, adopt inclusivity, and practice integrity, creating room for authentic camaraderie in the workplace.

3. Through years of working in various industries with different sizes & types of organizations, I understood which type of organization I would want to work for. I always found myself working for growth mindset companies more often than not. That said, it doesn't mean that no challenges are encountered in these organizations where a growth mindset is actively practiced. For example, challenges may come from the customer's team environment and cross-functional teams. This led me to think that organization-wide, one cannot distinguish whether it is a growth mindset company. That depends on which group or team you work with. I got to experience this during my tenure working with a big tech giant. I resonated with the organization's values, culture, and business, but during the first couple of months after starting the job, I realized I had made a mistake. The team I was part of strictly followed a fixed mindset, lesser known to my surprise, and I was completely functioning on an opposite plane. In the team, a culture

of avoiding mistakes, not being good enough, knowing it all, manipulations, deceit, undue credit taking, unhelpful conversations, and dishonesty was an everyday practice that proved non-conducive to keep up with exercising a growth mindset at work. I could sail through my time focusing on the work at hand, driving value for the customers, expanding my network to other growth mindset teams & collaborating with them, and contributing to the community that cared about working towards a common goal. That saved me! But was it ideal? No. From my past experiences, I had built tenacity, resilience, and perseverance while developing a growth mindset, which helped immensely. Some would say it is growing thick skin or maturing as a professional, but I beg to disagree. It's not just the environment that matters. Still, it takes conscious effort, full attention, commitment, positive self-belief, and more from oneself to continue developing a growth mindset. I felt the transformations I went through at every stage. Eventually, it empowered me to see that evolution is necessary for living a happy, fulfilled life by exercising your full potential. In this specific experience, Intrapreneurship brought me meaning, honor, and respect for myself & others.

4. Rewarding and recognizing efforts over outcomes can make a huge difference in making teams feel included in the workplace. When efforts are focused on improving something or doing it differently, the optimism it generates within teams is unmatched by any motivation. The free space, without fear of failure or punishment, allows teams to think creatively, innovate, solve problems, and improve. When organizations grow at scale, they face challenges with staying innovative. This is largely due to a lack of support for efforts accountability and more focus on outcomes. Encouraging this one simple fact, organizations or teams can empower their workforce to take more risks, experiment often, and innovate. Outcome-focused organizations become conservative in their approach, thinking, and the value they bring to their customers. Cultivating support for accountability of efforts over outcomes

needs conscious hard work, which can be practiced if organizations or teams start to shift their thinking & reward efforts more often.

5. I often missed a constructive voice of support, unwavering faith that 'I'll be able to get through,' and a mentor vested in my growth. I sought this kind of support many times as I didn't know what was good for my progress and what goals could influence my customers' success, but I did not find any avenues. Modern-age managers or team leads can play such dual roles. The role of being a business manager, reporting manager, and a skills cultivating coach (not a trainer). When managers remain primarily for tracking business and promotion management, they are neither effective leaders nor helping in growing the team for impact longevity. Organizations can redefine the roles of managers to include such responsibilities and have tightened accountability around them. This is a win-win proposition for hiring, cultivating, and retaining a skilled workforce to achieve the best bottom line. The effects on the bottom line of organizations vested in fostering a growth mindset can be summed up with this quote from Richard Branson: *'You take care of your employees, and they'll take care of your customers.'*.

While the environment encompasses team members, managers, leaders, communities, the reward culture, etc., this collectively supports cultivating a growth mindset. At the same time, there are things that individuals can apply to accelerate building their growth mindset. Contrary to popular belief, 'Only a few unique individuals can develop a growth mindset.'; most of us go through a fixed mindset at some point in our lives with few things but can develop a growth mindset for many other things. Here are some ways, if adopted, it can help individuals develop a growth mindset.

1. Increasing tolerance for errors, pace, and incremental progress.
2. Knowing and spotting what can and needs to be developed.
3. Constructive feedback with adequate resources and support.
4. Time dedicated to supporting each other.

5. Preparing the brain. An optimal level of performance stress can be a helpful motivator for developing a growth mindset.
6. Building a positive narrative around the learning experiment. For example, answering how the experiment outcomes will be helpful on a scale of community or humanity.
7. Build your reward system. Reward yourself even if you are experimenting with mundane things.
8. Surpass self-doubt.
    a. Practice writing three positive statements against one negative thought that comes up.
    b. Write a letter addressing someone else why the growth mindset is beneficial.
    c. Aim for incremental progress.

By and large, a growth mindset can be cultivated in many of us. Growth is a question of showing persistence and perseverance through a process to overcome hardship. It is about problem-solving and sustaining incremental progress that results in the short & long-term success of individuals and organizations. If the outlook of an organization, group, or team is only towards generating the bottom line numbers for their business, then that's a short-term strategy that needs much attention. These strategies must redefine themselves by making space to adopt new growth models.

Practice time. Let's get to it!

Answer the discovery questions below and reflect on your answers to devise a strategy that can work in the context of your current team. Take a resolve to make at least one or two changes out of the answered questions as a priority to work towards and experiment with your current team.

1. Individuals
    a. Are you experiencing a fixed or growth mindset?
    b. If the answer is a fixed mindset, start practicing the techniques mentioned below.
        i. Find an accountability partner within your team to receive constructive feedback.
        ii. Give and seek support to team members by following the 15-minute act of selfless service rule.
        iii. Open up to understanding the outcome of your work and its intended impact (beyond monetary implications).
        iv. Train your brain to prepare to see any problem as an opportunity by focusing on the problem in the present moment and identifying the parts where you'll need external help & support. Also, to repurpose the outcome as a higher target to achieve or something intangible (not relating to numbers, tags, etc.), remind yourself there is no shame, guilt, fear, or insecurity of any kind to worry about. It's just another task to learn from.
        v. Setting time to work on the problem independently without distractions and immersing yourself in the experience. 20 to 25-minute sprints have worked well for many types of work, keeping the creative & motivational triggers of mind in balance. Learn more about this through the Pomodoro technique.

vi. As far as possible, keep your body clean and less exposed to neurotoxins like caffeine, smoke, alcohol, medications, etc. Keep yourself hydrated with spring water and fed organic, clean food.

vii. Additionally, check practices mentioned in *Chapter - Collaboration, Teamwork & Allyship*.

c. If the answer is a growth mindset, then explore further. Identify if any learnings mentioned in this chapter can help you adopt a new way of functioning as an individual, within a group, a team, or an organization. Is there any area you'd like to develop your fixed mindset? If yes, then continue with the previous step.

2. Managers or Leaders

Ask yourself and identify areas to work towards. Questions with the answer 'No' make it to your list to work on.

a. Do you routinely support your team with time, resources, and adequate encouragement?

b. Do you stand by the team when they make mistakes and help them stay accountable?

c. Do you practice including team members by making no distinction in their contribution?

d. Do you believe your team members can achieve and develop a growth mindset? Yes or no, list your reasons for both; why?

e. Do you wish to support them in developing a growth mindset? Through your patience, constructive feedback, autonomy, and space to learn from their mistakes, practicing techniques to diffuse tension, not putting them on a pedestal every other time?

f. Do you have practices that reward efforts within a team?

g. Do you encourage team members to find time and space for additional collaborative work that can grow them professionally?

3. Organizations

    Ask yourself and identify areas to work towards. Questions with the answer 'No' make it to your list to work on.

    a. Do you have autonomy translated to teams to define their collaboration protocol?
    b. Do you have processes that are becoming bottlenecks for teams to function independently?
    c. Do you have managers who are also trained coaches with empathic abilities?
    d. Do you have processes to have managers and/or leaders stay accountable for their coaching outcome, growth of team members, and managing them with empathy?
    e. Do you have training and accountability structures for managers and/or leaders to help them practice inclusive & collaborative working teams?
    f. Do you have half-yearly or yearly retrospective cycles for improving your processes related to teams and their optimal functioning & feedback gathering?
    g. Do you have different processes catering to business disciplines like sales, marketing, product development, professional services, consulting services, etc.? Every discipline will have its rigor and needs based on the customer base, industry domains, and skills required to match the customer outcomes for effective service delivery.

CHAPTER 3

Accountability

'Accountability breeds responsibility.'

- Stephen Richards Covey, American Educator, Author, Businessman, and Speaker

I magine a world where

- There is no one other than yourself to whom you are answerable.
- There is nothing that makes you think if the outcomes are good or bad.
- There is no one who blames you for your wrongdoing.
- There is no one who shames you for committing mistakes.
- There is no one who stops you from learning and growing continuously.
- There is nothing that stops you from being curious.

Welcome to the world of accountability! Without accountability, humans would not have improved themselves through generations and made this world a better place to live. Thinking of accountability exists at two levels: professional and personal.

Professional Accountability

Professional accountability relates to owning one's work deliverables, defined goals, and outcomes as responsibilities to create value or impact on the organization, business, customers, or society. As part of any retrospective exercise, professionals can be appropriately questioned to provide details on what is working. This can ensure a safe space for everyone to learn, improve, and regularly deliver quality outcomes.

Personal Accountability

Personal accountability relates to owning your end of responsibility towards exhibited behaviors, taking a compassionate take on it, and improving the situation through learning every time, e.g., when one encounters obstacles, exercising the attitude of problem-solving rather than complaining or lamenting; when one is self-empowered to find a solution (either by themselves or through seeking adequate support) and work through it.

For a realistic professional, it's easy to follow this through. Where do we see a problem here? It sounds pretty straightforward. To your surprise, more often than not, this doesn't fit well because of many reasons. When some teams and professionals work together, they can encounter barriers like (a modified version of Apple's Directly Responsible Individual - DRI)

- Not having to know their domain of influence or authority to execute.
- Not having well-defined accountability around tasks or goals.
- Not getting a good environment - time, resources, and support needed to execute things.
- Having blurred boundaries of shared responsibilities.
- Not having enough will or motivation to stay accountable.
- Not having shared professional work ethics.

These things make or break the difference between well-working accountability within a team and not. The issue goes further down to needing a model or structure to keep accountability in check through recurring review cycles. Also, a second level of issue comes when a psychologically safe environment is not present to encourage the practice of personal accountability. I.e., when professionals encounter environments that promote perfectionism over incremental progress, knowing it all over continuously learning, fixed knowledge versus being curious. If the mindsets of perfectionism, knowing it all, and fixed knowledge are encouraged in any environment along with inadequate authority, then the outcome is likely mediocre.

- Outcomes that result in personal behaviors like shaming or blaming others for incomplete results.
- Not able to keep objectivity, stay curious, and conduct an open-minded retrospective exercise so that everyone learns collectively from mistakes.
- Not knowing what to improve upon and keep learning. This can be a big challenge for professionals who are held accountable but need to be provided with constructive feedback, objective feedback, and strategies to build upon their strengths & growth areas.
- Also, it's essential to note that the value provided to the organization, business, or customer greatly suffers when professionals encounter different practicing values & their self-interest is put first without concern for the interest of others. In such situations, professionals often say,

    o 'It's not my problem to deal with. Let's focus on the task at hand.'.
    o 'At my level, no one cares about the company's Vision & Mission.'.
    o 'This won't get caught as my goals are not tracking values I practice.'.

Well-executed accountability plays a greater role in keeping such intentional or unintentional ignorant personal behaviors in check. What can be useful is drawing a healthy boundary through well-defined role clarity &

responsibility frameworks. Those can help professionals deliver desired & valued service regularly. Most organizations and individuals would focus largely on professional accountability and the least on personal accountability (as it is deemed to be exercised), not knowing there is a symbiotic relationship between them. When addressed, we have better models to keep ourselves in check now and then. The success of defined & adopted accountability structures or models within an organization depends on individuals practicing them. In this context, personal accountability plays a bigger role in ensuring that professional accountability is attained with the least resistance. What can be done to improve the practice of personal & professional accountability?

1. Most organizations and teams have their model to exercise accountability practices. For instance, you may conduct regular outcome review meetings with leads, managers, or leaders. You may encourage documenting findings and setting expectations of needed support. You may have pre-defined guidelines for any issue resolution. You may have periodic reviews of maintaining & re-adjusting the accountability models as needed, making them more contextualized to suit an effective delivery of outcomes. Also, owning how you execute tasks helps here. Teams can use the RACI (Responsible, Accountable, Consulted, Informed) matrix to sophisticatedly chart professional accountability, tailor-made to fit their business function, group, or team.

2. Every professional can keep themselves in check by asking self-exploratory questions. Answers to these questions have the power to steer anyone in a more realistic, receptive, and positive direction, which develops personal accountability. One can practice this weekly, keeping a log of every week and taking necessary action to address them. Small actions taken through showing courage, openness, empathy, and patience can lead one to build everlasting trust. Which in itself makes a great foundation for professional accountability.
    a. Am I holding myself accountable?

- b. Am I holding others accountable when I should have?
- c. Am I blaming others?
- d. Am I shaming others by any means of behavior or words?
- e. Am I knowing the answers to these and still resisting? What is the reason for that?
- f. Am I holding back on having crucial & open conversations with others about what's okay and not?
- g. Am I open to keeping any assumptions at bay and staying curious to learn new, relevant information?
- h. Am I ready to spend the energy needed to hold myself back or choose to be vulnerable in my communication?
- i. Am I building or losing trust by doing what I know doesn't serve to be truly accountable?

3. Introducing a personal accountability model in a team. Encourage yourself and your colleagues to list behaviors catering to specific work styles and cultures. This can show how you and your teammates or colleagues would like to organize themselves concerning personal accountability. Each behavior can be something one is willing to do, be held accountable for doing, and hold others accountable for doing.

4. Commitment to purpose and mission demands a great amount of accountability. Managers helping teams understand the relevance of their individual goals and tasks to the company's vision and mission could be a good starting point. It's a great investment to keep the team motivated, involved, engaged, and included in the organization where they spend most of their hours. Encouraging teams to dive deep and ask questions to bring early clarity can help team members be more vested in the process and encouraged to drive ownership.

5. Most organizations have well-laid-out processes for critical functions around recruiting and retaining the workforce, like promotions and hiring processes. Organizations can minimize the

bureaucracies involved specifically with these processes by introducing tightened accountability models, especially exercised at the point of decision-making, i.e., by leaders, managers, or any other decision-makers. There are malpractices in the workforce to consciously make a note of, e.g., finding loopholes in the processes lacking accountability and misusing them to their undue advantage. For example, requiring to have a godfather or a godmother at the workplace to get promotion-related favors. Or not having a diverse interview panel for hiring or addressing the accountability gap in managers' goals to support unjust favoritism and advance their agendas over achieving collective success. Such bureaucracies do exist and are frequently practiced in organizations as they scale. To keep the process more objective and just, introducing more neutral evaluators, diluting authority by spreading it over a group of individuals rather than keeping it concentrated on a single individual or role, bringing in a reasonable amount of data points to support constructive outcomes, and defining goals more thoughtfully can be exercised on priority, respectively.

The outcome of such a focused & collective action to exercise appropriate accountability makes daily work responsibilities flow seamlessly. It can build up the foundation of trust, credibility, integrity, and self-assurance within teams. Resulting in professionals showing less resistance to faulty personal accountability, legitimately working through their professional accountability, and voluntarily raising their hands for increased responsibility.

Practice time. Let's get to it!

1. Individuals
   Practice building personal accountability.
   a. Answer all the questions mentioned in this chapter before and after every weekly team meeting you may have.
   b. Identify definitive actions and assign them time and place to execute them.
   c. Commit to practicing this as often, i.e., whenever you self-reflect and find accountability gaps.

2. Teams
   a. Managers or leaders can be proactive in setting up time to make team and individual goals more relevant to the vision & mission of the organization or for relevant customer outcomes. Setting a quarterly, bi-yearly, or yearly frequency could keep high momentum in teams to stay on course to achieve them.
   b. Set up a few member teams who can formulate & exercise a personal accountability model in a team.
   c. Devise largely just accountability models & review processes for business groups or teams in critical functions like hiring, promotions, opportunities to resource mapping, goals alignment, etc. Identify areas that need work from the guidance covered in this chapter.

3. Organizations
   a. Encourage the creation of psychologically safe environments across an organization through group-based communities. Provide adequate resources to promote knowledge sharing, reward efforts, etc.
   b. Devise largely just accountability models & review processes for critical functions like hiring, promotions, opportunities to resource mapping, goals alignment, etc. Identify areas that need work from the guidance covered in this chapter.

CHAPTER 4

Collaboration, Teamwork & Allyship

*'Individual commitment to a group effort.
That is what makes a team work, a company work, a
society work, a civilization work.'*

- Vince Lombardi, American Football Coach

I thought to myself, 'Here it is, that's my dream team! And this is how it feels to be part of.'.

It was one of the most challenging engineering project work we had ourselves as a team. Being one of the finest financial institutions in Europe, the client made it all the more inspiring for us to deliver a valued & good quality product. The team had every role and responsibility charted out. From a manager, leads, developers, quality assurance engineers, reviewers, and internal stakeholders to whom we would showcase our most valued contribution for their feedback. All the processes were set, and we followed all the stages of the software project management lifecycle from requirements to production rollout of our product. The team was innately devoted, and the best of the lot came together to live this dream journey for the next six months. Like much other work, we faced many challenges of an ever-changing scope of work, slipping milestones, research work going out of projected timelines, not having enough software resources to do testing, making makeshift adjustments, hoping that the product would work in a replica production environment, etc. Every now and then, we had it all going wrong. But still, it felt like a smoother journey than I had ever imagined. I asked myself, why?

The answer was in team collaboration, teamwork, and allyship. I thought I understood the difference between the three, but what I had understood before was far from the truth. I can now fathom why teams like these are called 'Dream Teams' to work with. The feelings of that environment are etched in the memory, the humble, lightened experiences are etched in the mind, and have had a lasting impact. Teamwork is the backbone of any organization. Without which there is no attempt of any success. The interconnected nature of humans comes to life with this organizational construct of a team, which spins up teamwork, collaboration, and allyship. The dream team sits at the intersection of the three. Refer to illustration *Relationship of Collaboration, Teamwork & Allyship to Dream Team*.

Teamwork
Members of the team are designed to follow a set of roles & responsibilities, and most likely, the responsibilities are independently done, and part of the work overlaps working with other team members to make it to the finish line. Teamwork is not limited to working sideways (with a peer group) but extends to work effectively upwards and downwards. Most likely, peer groups here are categorized based on the experience level in a subject matter.

Collaboration
Collaboration is an integration of different work responsibilities where boundaries of accountability have less overlap between them. Work responsibilities are crisply defined and harmoniously followed through. Effective feedback sharing, retrospective, and open, honest communication are the key to driving successful collaboration. There is no place for blame-

shifting, shaming, hoarding credit, focusing on only self-interest, and lacking concern for the interest of others. Essentially, they respect each other's time, efforts, contributions, accountability, and responsibilities while working on a common goal and sharing their expertise. Collaboration is seen within and across different teams or groups within an organization.

Allyship

Allyship is about showing a higher degree of integrity towards oneself and others. Practicing genuine behaviors of harmonious give & take, standing up for the right things, making space for others and yourself, and a win-win attitude to reconcile choices for the benefit of everyone involved. For the most part, this means staying empathetic towards each other, practicing authentic communication, and opening up your time to support others. That's allyship at work. But another essential component of allyship is active in an individual's personal space. Your family, home environment, friends, beliefs, and thoughts all collectively form allyship in the personal arena. This is most important to drive suitable mental space for anyone to offer reciprocal allyship at work; as they say, 'What you have received is what you can give!'.

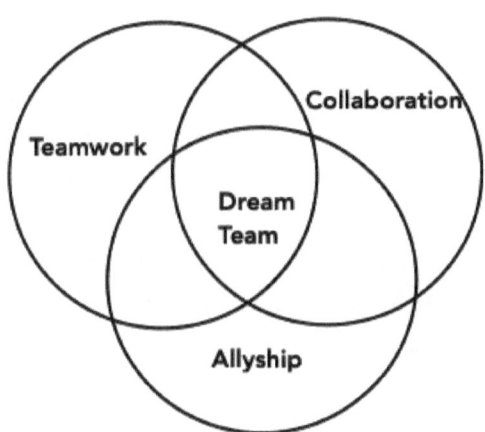

Relationship of Collaboration, Teamwork & Allyship to Dream Team

The dream team mattered as it gave a lot to us, i.e., our mindsets to keep us motivated, persist in efforts for long, persevere & endure without malice, work with quality, and drive productivity. It also helped all of us in our psyche to cultivate more creativity & innovative thinking (not Jugad!), cultivate harmonious reciprocity, build patience, have an open mind towards different perspectives, and practice empathetic, assertive communication. Does all of it sound familiar? It's not just the dream of any team member to have such a team to work with; any manager, leader, organization, or customer also welcomes it. Because it also drives the direct bottom line. Do such dream teams exist? Maybe that's not the question to ask. The important question is, most of the time, what are the challenges faced or obstacles seen to replicate a dream team in practice? Some of the notable obstacles that we often experience but do not notice or shrug away as if they aren't important are:

- Interpersonal communication barriers within a team
    - Assumptions of information regarding events.
    - Preceding conversations or any deliberations with assumptions.
    - Withholding information or sharing partial, incorrect, unclear information in communication.
    - Lack of interest or resistance to communicating better to avoid understanding gaps.
    - Negative hearsay experiences about the team or team members or anything related to the work at hand.
    - Idle talks over effective communication.

- Lack of autonomy to voice concerns within a team
    - Overt respect for hierarchical cultures.
    - Lack of authority to exercise assertiveness.

- Lack of mutual reciprocation of key attitudes within a team
    - Respect.
    - Trust.
    - Acknowledgement, Appreciation, and Recognition.

Collaboration, Teamwork & Allyship

- o   Support for mutual growth.
- o   Elevation in role, position, and opportunities.
- o   Inclusion to create a psychologically safe space for being vulnerable.

- Differences within a team
    - o   Unresolvable point of view.
    - o   Adopting resolution techniques or approaches.
    - o   Adapting to different personality traits like active, passive, aggressive, silent, or agnostic.
    - o   A stark gap in work ethics, beliefs, and held values.

Many may argue that these problems are difficult to solve or that they have the least power to influence the situations causing them. But there are possibilities that, if practiced well, they can be avoided, addressed, and resolved in the long run. After all, it's time well spent for having a smoothly functioning team at work.

1. Practices to overcome interpersonal communication barriers within a team.
    a. Breaking the ice early on. Let the team meet and bond in an informal setting before the start of any work together. Impersonal connections make it better for team members to help know each other, discard presumptions about one another, open a free communication channel, and form easier connections. Knowing what everyone holds as their unique values and talents can help team members encourage each other and know who to reach out to when any team member seeks help.
    b. Encouraging communication training within teams. Most professionals learn formal communication skills on their own throughout their careers. The advantage of informally improving communication is that team members stay curious to adapt to what works in the team, and the organization only has to invest a little in their growth

journey as this skill will be deemed developed as they go along. Formal indoor training on communication protocols matching personality types and effectively using various communication channels (verbal, written, face-to-face, online meeting, formal, informal), which can help collaborate team members better, is something every team and/or organization must prioritize. The effects of such training are strong and act as a great supplemental knowledge to improve the discernment of team members to practice effective communication as the situation demands.

2. Practices to overcome lack of autonomy to voice concerns within a team.
    a. Leaders, managers, and team leads can help take the initiative within the team, clearly set up communication protocols, and empower their teams to speak up.
    b. The most critical practice to follow is to stay away from compliance or punishment culture. When team members are met with protocols of complying with certain rigid and hard standards or fear getting punished for speaking up, the innate sense of openness and flexibility is diminished. Encouraging free-flowing and respectful communication is everyone's job, and it starts with leaders being an example of practicing it themselves, infusing lightness and a sense of acceptance in their surroundings. Nothing sticks better than having a humble role model.
    c. Taking frequent time breaks during the workday to carry out informal talks with team members and often showing up informally also helps signal the accepting culture of open communication, where everyone can participate, maintaining healthy boundaries and mutual respect.

3. Practices to overcome the lack of mutual reciprocation of key attitudes within a team.

a. Mutual reciprocation attitudes are key for having team members live without a burden on them, without experiencing the feelings of being exploited, cheated, pushed over, and disrespectful of their time & efforts. Instead, they focus on the real business problem at hand and find effective solutions for them. In comparison, some teams can easily practice mutual reciprocation and set a good precedent. Others can also project that these are just another set of principles that works 'by chance' within a team and are not worth paying attention to as it can take some of their efforts away from delivering a business outcome. But this approach soon backfires on teams who do not innately practice few or all mutual reciprocation attitudes, i.e., respect, trust, acknowledgment, appreciation, and recognition. Accepting that these are important foundational attitudes one must continuously try to cultivate, and they outweigh the time one thinks is wasted developing them. What is considered to be taking away their time from achieving business outcomes soon becomes why they spend additional hours resolving team interpersonal conflicts or staying dissatisfied with the working dynamics. Achieving business goals is a direct function of satisfaction amongst team members and bringing their best selves to work. These attitudes bring the best out of everyone on the team. Accepting this and resolving to work towards developing them is the first and the most difficult step for many. But it must be taken.

b. Secondly, team members can practice being supportive, openly acknowledging each other's wins more often, appreciating small acts of success amongst themselves, recognizing team members doing more than just business as usual (BAU) tasks, and inspiring others to join hands & share opportunities amongst each other. Having honest, polite communication, along with a 5-minute practice of selfless acts, builds trust among team members.

c. Respecting each other can be hard for many team members for many reasons, for example, belief mismatch, valuing different things, etc. Still, one can start with the fundamental understanding that someone's experience, level, position, power, status, credibility, and persona have nothing to do with being deserving of the most basic level of human respect. This must be exercised. If not, to the least, everyone can show humility and be forthcoming to accept instances when they failed to exhibit respect towards others.

d. Inclusion has always been a tricky thing to accept. Some may say that you only feel included as much as you open yourself to others, and others may argue that inclusion is an intentional act of skill to practice. Practice both and see which one works in the context of the team you are working with. As the team changes, new ways of adopting new information must change. Keeping a psychologically safe space, which is open for all, is also possible when individuals are allowed to bring in their vulnerable selves at work without being exposed to shame, guilt, fear, or instigating insecurity that negatively impacts their position, job, or image. One can start by looking at every instance and every conversation as if they are starting afresh (without carrying the baggage of what they know already). This can be hard to practice at first, but if done repeatedly and incrementally, focusing on human empathy (less on the business problem at that instance) increases the chances of success.

e. Recognizing shame-inducing behaviors within the team. The hidden shame within an organization creates obstacles for teams to be their best selves and be innovative, build trust, and exercise respectful professional connections amongst each other. Such hidden shame can be vigilantly recognized when team members showcase some of the

Collaboration, Teamwork & Allyship

behaviors like unjustified back-channeling, blaming, bullying, comparisons, unjustified cover-ups, discrimination, favoritism, gossiping, harassment, perfectionism, one-upping, self-worth tied to excessive productivity, teasing, etc.

f. One can also devise a marble bowl game for the team to build mutual trust. More often than not, teams work in a space where they can reach each other and meet often during their day. Every team member can practice adding one marble to an empty bowl (at the beginning) when they do anything, which results in gaining the trust of another team member. At the same time, remove a handful of marbles when they do anything, resulting in losing a team member's trust. The empty bowl shows the team can work towards building more trust amongst themselves as a priority. The filled bowl recognizes the amount of trust that already exists within the team, giving a calibration for what to work towards. This can give team members an immediate calibration and focus on their interpersonal relationships, negatively affecting collaboration at work. Reminding them to re-shift some efforts to build trust within the team intentionally.

g. Keeping teams self-motivated to collaborate effectively requires team members to work on common goals that they agree on for most parts and get engaged early in the planning and accountability-setting process. Any differences of opinion can be resolved early on, giving the team a sense of relief so that they can work with less friction during the sprints of deliverables.

h. Teams can also practice devising communication techniques for their work products. This could include using the right tools, which impose fewer distractions, etc. Suppose most of their time and resources are consumed on keeping unrelated communication ongoing. In that case, they will be less motivated to communicate openly or focus on their task.

i. Appreciation and recognition can be done as a team-wide exercise, keeping the element of pleasant surprise. It can be practiced randomly as an act of acknowledgment. Showing these on a board where sticky notes are visible to all team members can be a good motivator for building mutual trust. It can make team members feel valued by each other. Every team member can also practice writing about their day's positive experiences as they come or leave from work. For instance, colored sticky notes can reflect their feelings: green - hearty, orange - elevated, yellow - happy, red - excited, white - neutral. Such small practices make everyone feel included, appreciated immediately, noticed, and valued, and bring in trust to open up & show up every day with their authentic selves. It can also help gauge the team's morale and see if any adjustments need to be made to improve it.

j. Creating and sharing opportunities, either as part of a common interest community or publishing it on a commonly accessible notice board, helps everyone feel included. Everyone can be empowered to be considered for equally participating in or raise their interest in taking on more responsibilities for further professional growth.

k. Building communities for a common purpose within the team and spending 5 percent of their time nurturing and growing the community actively can help team members or employees stay connected with what they enjoy the most while creating value. It can also help find meaning in joining hands and participating with teams more often. This also creates a great opportunity for team members to know each other more deeply and positively. Taking a step forward in building innate trust and autonomy amongst themselves.

4. Practices to overcome differences within a team.
    a. Empower team members to ask objective questions without raising blame or judgments. Cultures lead to self-empowered team members only if there is no fear of meeting with dire consequences of exercising objective curiosities. This is also a function of how well-enforced compliance or punishment culture is discouraged within teams or groups in an organization. The higher the practice of such armed leadership, the lesser the chances of teams staying objective.
    b. Teams can intentionally practice to gain a different perspective. Regardless of their role, every team member can be tied with accountability partners. Who meets weekly with each other and exercises open dialogue to raise any noticed blind spots. They can discuss any episodes that need to be viewed differently.
    c. Teams can plan ahead to put efforts into devising different solutions. They can seek help from a peer or support from a senior professional or mentor if and when required. Teams can experiment with solutions, giving them a chance & space to be more open to challenging their perspectives. Working openly with others to welcome & accept a different point of view can build muscle within team members to be more accommodating of different viewpoints as they deem fit. Teams can put in some effort and see if the results are making a difference, and carry out a retrospective exercise to identify areas where the team seeks more information, support, time, or resources to get better results next time. Teams can empower themselves to take their needs to the right individuals in a team with the authority to provide adequate support.
    d. As a team, log the results of such experiments and share any new practice that comes up as a result of it. Spread it by sharing it with other organizational groups or teams to adopt effective collaboration protocols.

e. Managers or leaders can encourage & support teams to share such insights and processes, showcasing an example that personal growth is a part of professional work deliverables and effective outcomes. And that soft skills like communication or cultivating values of respect, trust, etc., are accounted for and acknowledged.

Having a team environment where we all feel like coming back to every single day, contributing openly without the fear of being pushed over, welcoming each other as their best selves, promoting & supporting each other's work, sharing opportunities without being fearful of undue competitiveness, building mutual trust, etc. is what a dream team encompasses. It may sound like a lot to take on, but in reality, that is what we all truly aspire to have within our teams. It matters to make living our realities worthwhile and have memorable experiences on our journey; that is what matters to us: harmoniously working together, collaborating, and being each others' allies.

Practice time. Let's get to it!

1. Individuals, Teams
    a. Identify one or two practices against each below-mentioned area (from the list mentioned in this chapter) you'd like yourself or your team to work towards.
        i. Interpersonal communication barriers.
        ii. Lack of autonomy to voice concerns.
        iii. Lack of mutual reciprocation to essential attitudes.
        iv. Resolving differences within a team.
    b. Devise any three micro-strategies from what is listed here or brainstorm more within the team to identify what suits them best.
    c. Practice, Practice, Practice!
    d. Conduct an experiment for at least 4 to 6 weeks or more.
    e. Meanwhile, engage with team members to see a difference in their engagement. Organizations most widely use surveys to track such outcomes, but it risks making the entire experience mechanical, inauthentic, and heartless. The best results are seen when you see impromptu results. For example, different colors for mood-mapped sticky notes are posted on the wall. For instance, green is hearty, orange is elevated, yellow is happy, red is excited, and white is neutral. This can frequently show individuals' feelings and directly reflect changes within the team, which most surveys fail to capture effectively.
    f. If one experiment works, then on to the next one!

2. Organizations
    a. Identify which behaviors are predominantly stopping teams or business groups from practicing openness, healthy collaboration over unhealthy competition, and unempathetic teamwork. Conduct regular in-person training to address these behaviors.
    b. Realign performance measurement process by conducting reviews to factor in the field learnings that support positive,

conducive behaviors for promoting collaboration, teamwork, and allyship.

PART III

Living the Dream!

> *'All our dreams can come true if we have courage to pursue them.'*
>
> *- Walt Disney, American Animator, Film Producer, and Entrepreneur*

If you are alive, then you are made of desires, wishes, and dreams! Those are so close to your heart that one asserts themselves throughout their lives to fulfill them. Everyone wants to be a winner, a success story, and live their dreams leaping beyond their current realities. More often than not, these individuals can have the most significant impact within their organizations, teams, their surrounding environments, and within themselves. They are the *Stars*!

Someone who knows that business function or experience-led impact always stands secondary compared to the impact driven by their performance & innate passion. These professionals do not sweat to take on more responsibilities and are open to holding up accountability. It might seem that they magically know when, what, and how to give energy to something that needs their attention. And deliver an impact that is either directly aligned with the organization's outcomes or indirectly looking out for its long-term interests. They do it all gracefully with utmost integrity.

Everyone should want to invest in professionals who will do what they think is right, whether permitted to do it, showing the required legitimate courage towards their pursuits.

This is what it takes for those who want to start *Living the Dream* and making it their new reality, transforming themselves through rational and sustainable change.

How can one become a *Star* and transform from living their realities into living their dreams?

CHAPTER 5

Having it All!

'The key to happiness is having dreams...'

- James Allen, British Philosophical Writer

There you go. What comes to mind when you see these words, 'Having it All!'?

- 'It's impossible!'
- 'Maybe, one day!'
- 'Not sure, how?'
- 'Even if one has it all, can one sustain it all?'

One can be happy to have it all and anxiously think about what if I lose it all the next moment. The perplexity of having success so close, what if it goes away? Sooner, one realizes that they are overthinking it! Having it all is a momentary game of chance and luck, and that's not how reality works; that's not how life works. In life, you have stop-gaps. You have complex, grueling, and excruciatingly painful challenges to accept & live by. Most of us may have thought about these situations and played them over many times. Some of us have experienced them several times and have self-doubt. Can everyone have it all? Can everyone do it all?

The real question is, what does it mean for YOU to "Have it All?".

And the answers are different for different individuals. We all aspire for it somewhere in our life, whether it be our family, job, friendships, money, relationships, the next big thing, the next significant role, the subsequent big success, etc. Starting to think about what it means to you to have it all is the key to understanding whether it is possible.

Yes, having it all is possible!

In your context, in your time, in your capacity, in your circumstances! Everything is possible but not at once, not at a given time but over a timespan. That hope is not false. I have seen it happen many times in my professional and personal life. And around me in others' lives as well. Anyone with the mindset of a champion, the language of an excellent communicator, and the ability to find the right opportunities, along with appropriate action, resolve, patience, and resilience, can have it all. One may say I do not have these qualities; does it mean I cannot have it all? In that case, what's next for me?'. It can be accessed by anyone as a structured process, starting with identifying what living a realistic dream looks like for you.

1. Define your dreams.
    a. Set ambitious goals. Ambitious enough to induce some fear or scare within you.
    b. They are challenging to achieve but not impossible. Some pre-existing proof is available, reflecting that they are achievable.
    c. They align with what you are good at, what the world needs, and what the world values.

2. Break them down into milestones. Breaking it down gives it the meaning, focus, and clarity it needs.
3. Prioritize them and see what fits your responsibilities in your day, week, month, and year.
4. Define a more realistic timeline. If you want to achieve something great, commit to giving it your most precious thing: your time & commitment, an unbreakable resolve that follows through an action.
5. Strip down everything else from your priority list.
6. Now, re-look at the list and see if it has the potential to generate the desired outcomes to achieve your dream.

Talking of dreams could be a contextual question. Knowing what 'having it all' means to you, outlining your dreams is the first step. For example, if you think you can be an astronaut without a formal degree, that's different from the kind of dreams we are discussing. Dreams that are seemingly impossible but realistically possible, e.g., In case you do not have a formal degree to become an astronaut, you can still work with astronauts provided you have specific skills developed that they need, which you can fill in for. Defining dreams is not a random process that contains artificial, unattainable, imaginative, illusory goals. If you are leading in this direction, then STOP! And recalibrate your compass of rationality and bring it back to earth. If you need help to do it yourself, follow the above process. If you still find yourself getting nowhere, it's time to find the right mentor or coach to help you navigate this puzzle. Unless this is not figured out, your chances of achieving much tangible success remain low.

Practice time. Let's get to it!

Individuals
1. Run through all the questions this chapter poses and curate answers based on your current or future aspirations. Knowing what is true for you is the first step in exploring whether you can have it all.
2. Follow through the process mentioned in the chapter to further outline how living a realistic dream will look like for you. Note it down with as much detail as you can, and read these daily or weekly.

CHAPTER 6

The Skills Game

'...The key to success is making dreams come true.'

- James Allen, British Philosophical Writer

'My skills are enough to get me to the next level. What matters is the bottom line. I call that a success!.'

We have heard and experienced these statements repeatedly in organizations & teams that focus highly on the outcomes and specifically only on the monetary & financial outcomes. Is there anything wrong with it? Yes and No. No, because every organization that works in business is deemed a for-profit organization, there is a focus on earning or being compensated for products or services they render to their customers. And Yes, because driving organizations and their work outcomes predominantly on account of financial uptake and revenue numbers is a short-term strategy of failure as it invites an unsustainable work culture that is cut-throat, bureaucratic, exhaustive, and dissatisfyingly unpleasant, which no rational individual prefers to be part of for a long run.

When it comes to long-term sustained success, organizations focus on the competence, i.e., performance and impact of teams in which they operate. And both are largely tied to many skills employees exhibit effectively in the work environment. It helps an organization sustain uncertainty, respond well to changing trends, and stay relevant. Skills that matter are measured in every organization through some tangible goals attached to work, but crucial skills should be measured and evaluated more often. Such skills work behind the scenes like our subconscious minds, i.e., knowing that it exists and taking all crucial final decisions for you but not actively present.

Today's world economies are highly concentrated on information sharing and largely work based on knowledge. It can easily be called a knowledge economy as that's where future growth and strength lie. Education has been such an integral part of human evolution through time immemorial. One who deeply wants to grow in today's fast-paced world often asks questions like,

- Does knowledge mean skills?
- Which is the most important skill to learn?
- How many skills do I need to bring success in my life?
- Where can I go to develop these skills?
- How do I know that I am developing new skills?

They are all valid and legitimate questions to those who care to skill themselves. The most important skill is knowing what to learn, how to learn it when to apply it, what to apply it to, and how much to apply it. Without the cultivation of this intelligence, any information can be considered futile and have no impact on drawing any useful outcomes. Having said that, there are also skills learned for the sheer joy of learning them, which induce a different state of satisfaction within oneself.

We invariably use many terms like skills, information, and knowledge interchangeably. Is there a real need to emphasize the difference between them? They all mean the same, don't they? Knowing their different nuances helps to understand how skills are developed. In today's age, it is more than normal to consume mere information in more quantity than we have ever before. The information fatigue is for real! Then how do we distill the one that is needed and save time from unnecessary information overload?

Information is not enough to develop skills! Translating the information into action and iteratively applying learning is what matters. On top of that, actions that result in useful outcomes are valued the most. Another way to understand these various terms is by understanding the stages of Skills Mastery. Skills Mastery is the continuum representing the different stages of maturity derived by the practice of using information, knowledge, and wisdom, focusing on how it translates into outcomes. Skills Mastery levels are different in how people use information, how they often utilize it in practice and correlate it to the intent & outcome they produce.

- Mastery Level 1: Talk the talk; skill boosts a superficial sense of knowledge; information is held statically.
- Mastery Level 2: Walk the talk; skills translate into practice and action, but results may or may not come forth.
- Mastery Level 3: Walk the walk, and their results do the talk; skills are transformed into knowledge, and results come forth.
- Mastery Level 4: Walk the walk & don't talk, but inadvertently, results do the talking; skills are transformed into knowledge, and results are seen and distilled widely. Takes the form of evolving wisdom as they result in a deeper expertise.

How do we get from mastery level 1 to mastery level 4?

By repetitive, persevered, patient action. We all want to continually and incrementally practice to reach mastery level 4, the highest level most desired by organizations, conducive for teams, and effective for individuals. But one may wonder, do we need all skills developed at the mastery level 4? The answer is subjective. It is situation and context-based. You may or may not be required to reach all skills at an expertise level 3 and/or 4. To understand which ones do, one should consider the essential skills discussed here for an individual's professional and personal growth. They apply to all; it could be a leader, a manager, or an individual contributor, agnostic of the role. Foremost are the skills that are the backbone of any job related to your functional role. The functional role means the primary field in which you work, and your job entails having deep knowledge about. For example, software development, software language coding, quality assurance testing, project management, finance, legal, human resources, marketing, etc. Your industry, technical domain, and business function collectively decide the overlap of skills, whether you need them or not & their importance. For example, in addition to functional skills, one may require formal academic education in the management discipline. Functional skills are non-negotiable for any job you apply for, are essential, and are used as part of your day job. They are cultivated and developed most likely through academic pursuits, on-the-job learning, or extensive workshops & training. Most organizations have goals aligned where these skills are inadvertently measured for the outcome they produce.

Other skills are less likely to be formally measured but are assessed by your interviewers, peers, leaders, managers, and customers. They are what I call helps in 'formally elevating your professional skills game.'. Let's run over them.

Learning how to learn
Learning how to learn, in itself, is a skill. When dealing with such a rapid pace of technological and business changes, there is a dire need to learn and develop new skills more swiftly than ever while enjoying the learning process. In such times, a way and an approach to learning gives one an added advantage of pace to achieve & produce better results for your organizations, industries, and customers. There is no other way out than being a perpetual learner. If not immediately, everything you learn eventually returns to you as the most considerable support you can seek when you need it. So, keeping at it is a good strategy for life. The most important thing this skill teaches you is how to be comfortable with the discomfort that learning brings. Learning is a complex process of gathering information, understanding the concepts, how - when - how much information to apply, and retrospectively learning from the experience. But it contains several cycles to address failure until you find a working solution. Going through these cycles, one can learn to be more resilient, determined, and handle discomfort by staying objective about the outcome & impact it produces rather than getting absorbed by and staying consumed in the

dissatisfaction of failures.

Growth Mindset

Refer to the discussion from *Chapter - Mindset* for cultivating a growth mindset.

Organizing Skills

Skills include knowing how to set goals, prioritize them, break them down into bite-sized achievable work packets, and execute them. Organizing one's goals can help optimize the resources one spends (time, funding, energy, etc.) effectively.

Manage everyday life aspects

- **Time & Energy**

    Time and energy are two resources that are the most valued, and always seem to have less of it. Especially considering today's knowledge economy demands everyone to be up-to-date with the latest and greatest information, achieve their desires, and tick their goals for success. Time can quickly run out amongst many existing distractions if one is not intentional about managing it. As mentioned below, a *2 by 2 Decision Matrix for Task Prioritization* can help identify how they spend their time doing which tasks. Write your goals and tasks in each quadrant as they fit based on your situation. Follow the quadrant guidance below to organize the resources assigned to those goals and tasks.

	URGENT	NOT URGENT
IMPORTANT	DO IT NOW	PLAN IT
NOT IMPORTANT	DELEGATE	DROP IT

    2 by 2 Decision Matrix for Task Prioritization - Eisenhower Decision Matrix

- **Goals prioritization**

    A crucial step in goal planning is goal prioritization. At a given point, one may have many things to line up to work on. Still, considering we have limited time, attention, focus, and energy resources, those who prioritize their goals are more motivated to stay on course for a long time. The above-mentioned *2 by 2 Decision Matrix for Task Prioritization* is a good starting point with an overlay of manually identifying how and which goals are better aligned to driving your success parameters; for example, some goals can make success faster but lack in quality, so one must deliberate on thought what factors are driving the successfully achieving goals and consider those factors to prioritize goals further.

- **High-stake decision-making**
  Every job entails decision-making. It's a non-negotiable skill for professionals to carry at any level. More important is the methodology followed for decision-making based on the gravity of the matter at hand. What that means is decision-making can quickly turn into posing risks or holding up high stakes if not done as intended. One can learn the skills of making high-stakes decision-making to move at a pace and remove obstacles effectively on the path to success. For example, the skill may include understanding protocols to follow, knowing the extent of value at stake, weighing your options carefully considering pros & cons, taking an outsider's viewpoint, looking at the situation from a different perspective, and finding innovative or creative solutions to pursue the subject of a problem.

- **Saying 'Yes' & 'No'**
  Saying 'Yes' could be easier for most of us when taking on work responsibilities that we are obliged to do. Many enjoy taking on additional responsibilities based on the outcome they want to achieve, and some are highly motivated by the impact it creates on customer value or their performance. Whatever the reason, does it mean taking additional responsibility is the only path to progression? Yes and No. Most likely, additional responsibility in the right arena can help professionals develop new skills through new experiences and provide exposure to challenging situations. But it can also pose additional unassumed fatigue and dissatisfaction if one is not managing

themselves better or is unaware of the amount of responsibility undertaken or responsibilities are not tied to any tangible short-term or long-term outcomes related to the work at hand. This is when professionals can learn to practice saying 'No.'. The practice of saying 'No' has picked up more momentum than ever in recent years. Why is that so? What has changed? Why is it encouraged more by Industrial and Organizational psychologists? The answer lies in many factors such as exhaustion by information overload, meeting fatigue, work-from-home culture invariably lets one take on more work, longer hours put in at work, continuous working without adequate intentional breaks, businesses demanding more outcomes and growth in a short period, rigorously growing culture of performance tied to business numbers outcome, lack of support from leaders & management to effective than more outcomes, and unharmonious accounts of give-take. This and more reasons add to the pressures of keeping the job and not leaving any stone unturned so that one can reach or avoid obstacles to the next promotion at work. Professionals readily succumb to saying 'Yes' rather than exercising rational thinking and actively pursue saying 'No' (gently professionally) to things that have the least impact or matters the least. Organizations and managers can very well identify when more responsibilities are piled on their best performers, and it'll keep them saying 'Yes' until they can't take more and start practicing saying 'No,' indicating enough is enough. Managers inadvertently practice this tactic when they want something to get done. They'll give responsibility to a busy person, as the chances of saying 'Yes' are higher because they get things done. But this can start posing an issue with the well-being of team members struggling to practice saying 'No' or having poor self-management skills. So managers, leaders, and team members must practice encouraging an environment where appropriate boundaries are laid out and saying 'No' to things is welcomed without getting judged, shamed, or punished. This can avoid employee dissatisfaction, having them taxing out of their energy sources, and an effective team collaboration by promoting good behaviors, i.e., not having to encounter difficult feelings of being a pushover, being a doormat, or over giving to others for selfless reasons. Many could also feel afraid to practice saying 'No' because when they say 'No' to something, they can be daunted by the new thing they are saying 'Yes' to. The unfamiliarity of the new world that saying 'No' brings can make many uncomfortable and remain in their ways to take more than they can manage. Seeking support from one's immediate team, cultivating self-management practices, and empowerment from managers and/or leaders can help professionals get over this obstacle. The practice of saying 'Yes' and 'No' is essential. Choosing either extreme is not conducive, but cultivating discernment of when to exercise what option can help professionals win in their daily lives and get better things done that matter.

- **Discern & Act on the right thing**
  Once identified and practiced saying 'Yes' or 'No' to things, one must practice further discernment to act on the task rightly. This entails professionals understanding the scope, boundaries, resources, authority, and accountability models attached to a task to perform the required action correctly.

- **Getting things done**
  Taking action on things does not necessarily mean that things are guaranteed to be done. Many professionals can get stuck in the process of overstretching themselves, i.e., needing to know when to take external help & ask for support. Many would get stuck in analysis paralysis mode, creating hindrances to the inertia required to move forward, and many would encounter a great motivation gap on their path. In contrast, many would just be new to the concept of what it means to get it done. Essentially, professionals understand the end goal for every task at hand and know what it means to say 'it got done,' define criteria for achieving the finish line, and understand the process to follow through it. Then, getting things done can be a fun process to follow through. The idea is to gain clarity as much as possible and early on. Open Pandora's box of relevant questions, clarify them through the right authority and gain insights early. This can give many advantages to individuals who always get things done and stay on course as they

know, have planned, and come prepared for most parts of what they need to take on today. Cultivate knowing how to ask the right questions and the right questions for the context. It can be done by observing team members who do this well, taking support from immediate managers or peers, seeking their guidance, and practicing at every chance. More than anything else, organizations, leaders, and managers appreciate and want professionals who exhibit this trait of 'Getting things done.' But most cherished and valued are those who 'Get things done' but the 'Right way.'

- **Right way**
Speaking of getting things done the right way is often understood as looking for perfection in your delivered outcomes. This is the biggest myth! Perfectionism may appear to dwell in the minds of those who seek unreasonable and excessively high standards for everything at every time. But that's not the domain of perfectionism. Perfectionism is an ever-evolving process that is never attainable, so, in reality, perfectionism is impossible to achieve or sustain healthily. Organizations, leaders, managers, customers, and team members, everyone included, know and expect nothing like a perfect outcome. What is often referred to as 'Doing things the right way' is the basis of emphasizing excellence over perfection and incremental progress over perfectionism. The quality outcome sets one aside who simply 'Gets things done' versus someone who 'Gets things done the right way.'. Appreciated by all, wanted by all, expected from all, but delivered by a few. Ironically, professionals' performance is often measured by just outcomes instead of by delivery of quality outcomes or excellence based on context. As it's difficult to track a measure of excellence in the performance of team members at every level, it's rather kept as an optional criterion to fill in most of the time. However, more often than not, organizations appreciate and hold on to professionals who practice this trait or do things well. What is important is that individuals develop an early understanding of the factors associated with delivering excellence. These factors may differ at the level of a task, goals, outcome, and impact. These are well understood in the context of team,

individual, organization, and customer impact. Developing this understanding at every level through peers, managers, and leaders can help manage one's goals better.

Communication

The key to human existence and our collective experiences relies on practicing basic forms of communication. It is essential and ingrained in our psyche and sets us apart from using one of our senses of speech in differentiation with animals. We can practice speaking, deeply comprehending words, and communicating a message to better understand each other along with the subject matter and make an adequate welcoming connection with people around us. Communication is key in our day-to-day lives to professional work success. More than just knowing its significance, cultivating how to communicate at work is essential. There are different facets of communication. Communication is the most important key to presenting your ideas, your thoughts, and your outcomes, and to build & showcase your credibility through personal branding. Communication that is most appreciated and welcomed in a professional environment is the one that is practiced for engagement with stakeholders, with a positive tone, assertiveness, empathetic language, and focus on positive objectivity. Other skills around communication that are important to develop are carrying out effective negotiation conversations that help in customer-facing roles, working with different disciplines of business teams, collaborative work with team members to derive a mutually agreed consensus, and creating Influence through written or verbal mode. It is observed that professionals who have their communication skills aligned properly exhibit more authority and self-respect and command respect from others around them. Practicing Nonviolent Communication (a communication model developed by Dr. Marshall Rosenberg) in a highly conflicting environment can develop and retain adequate empathy, disagree but commit to what is required to be done, and improve the quality of engagement among team members.

Personal Branding

Personal branding is commonly practiced in many geographies and cultures; in others, it is perceived as socially arrogant. Exhibiting and making propaganda of one's credibility & achievements in many cultures is considered to boost one's ego, diminishing one's humility quotient, being arrogant & prideful, and compromising the positive behavioral values one showcases around them. Others may feel threatened or intimidated if they misperceive the driver of personal branding. If it's such a negativity-bound act, then why is personal branding so important? The difference lies in the understanding of what personal branding means. Personal Branding is not about bragging or showing off your talents to the rest of the world so that you can elevate yourself to achieve a certain name tag, status, or momentary fame. It is a practice of actively keeping the world informed of new interventions, thoughts, ideas, innovation, etc., pursued by oneself to inspire and/or to collaborate (possibly get together) by showcasing their credibility, share & receive new perspectives as a matter of progression, and contribute by collectively coming together to make a wider impact on the world & realize their potential. It is an impact-driven community-building act practiced with a service mindset. With this in mind, personal branding changes the perspective of those who resist going out there and being a giver on an open platform rather than confiding in smaller spaces and limiting their true potential to serve others.

Leadership without a title
For many decades, the perceived meaning of leadership has been that there is one wo/man responsible for leading a pack of people and working towards attaining a single-minded goal for a larger good. This overly generalized definition, which is engraved in our minds through centuries of storytelling patterns, role models, and other mediums, limits a lot of us who felt that we were the leaders in our domain but never came forward to celebrate and share those traits to bring more good to the world, because they lacked title or authority to do so. In the corporate world, through the years, this definition has changed with time. Leadership is no longer about a select set of leaders with roles, titles, and positions following a hierarchical work culture (typically top-down organization management). But it goes beyond! Leadership is about creating a fellowship. Fellowship of people who follow a leader for their shared interests and not for the leader. Leaders who achieve this inspire with their common beliefs and mission to work

towards, i.e., the common good of human goals. We see many professionals who are self-inspired to create more individuals like them who believe in the company's vision and mission. These are great assets to the company as they create impact by being themselves and following what they think is right without needing anyone's authority, title, role, or permission to do what they do for a larger good. Such leaders, without titles, expand the definition of impact within and outside organizations. They are okay with being misunderstood for the longest time in order to do the right thing or something remarkably innovative. They are welcomed, encouraged, cherished, and supported most times, as this is one trait you either have in you or you don't. One can create many leaders by following training protocols over the years. But one can only create leaders who inspire others to become leaders themselves by just being themselves. That is harder to achieve through any training. It's an innate trait tied with deep human functioning of being comfortable within themselves, actively working on their inner self, showing bravery, exhibiting courage, and owning their vulnerabilities authentically. Organizations wanting to invest in professionals who can exhibit leadership without a title can focus on building the skill by

- Allowing exercising healthy boundaries and promoting being at ease.
- Adopting a perpetual learning attitude.
- Celebrate wins and celebrate milestones.
- Commitment to shared purpose.
- Defining, accepting, bringing out, and normalizing collective fear of uncertainty.
- Leading with empathy and vulnerability, healthy pursuits, and compassion for self & others. Here, vulnerability refers to deeply accepting one's vulnerabilities as strengths and using them appropriately. For example, honesty can be seen as a vulnerable quality to practice at many workplaces but can help build trust, alliances, and genuine community bonds.
- Normalizing working through their inner self. Leaping beyond their deep-seated insecurities and fears.

The Skills Game

- Practicing support while behaving adequately, stern yet soft.
- Practicing gratitude.
- Practicing kindness and giving hope.
- Practicing straightforward, objective, nonviolent communication.
- Practicing taking the right actions.
- Promoting belonging and inclusivity.
- Supporting adequate rest, fun, and health.
- Taking adequate risks.
- Welcoming diverse, unique, useful perspectives.

Behaviors

Behaviors conducive to a good collaborative environment can drive any organization's work culture and business impact. Most organizations have and follow successfully laid out good behaviors like professional communication, etiquette for internal & external engagements, interpersonal engagements, etc. On the surface level, these behavioral protocols are widely followed. But beyond these, in reality, unpleasant behaviors do exist and are practiced more regularly than one realizes. This can gravely affect the team's working dynamics and outcomes. They are ignored and intentionally unattended by leaders & managers more often than one knows, which ends up promoting what is widely termed as non-conducive or unhealthy work cultures. Professionals in such organizations know how to get by Human Resources processes through bureaucracies and by using their influential positions. Those professionals often hear themselves say, 'Behaviors have no bearing on my promotion!' , 'I/We don't have time for this.'. Unpleasant behaviors, a few mentioned below, when practiced, leave everyone around feeling uncomfortable, unpleasant, and stressed.

- (Borderline) Sexual harassment
- Bullying, shaming, name-calling, mocking.
- Deceit & manipulation, dishonesty. Misusing information at hand to further self-fulfilling intentions and objectives, lacking team, organization, or customer impact.
- Envying, not wishing well of others.

- Emotional Harassment.
- Hoarding or taking away credit.
- In-equanimity.
- Lack of integrity.
- Lack of respect towards oneself and others due to differences in backgrounds, education, experience, appearances, race, religion, sexual orientation/gender, disability, deformity, etc.
- Projecting their insecurities and fears on others.
- Succumbing to predefined thinking models, 'This is how it is. I can't help but to play it as it demands.' and joining hands with others to create multiplying effects of increasingly seen unpleasant behaviors.
- Treating others as a doormat or a pushover.

Some would consider such behaviors resulting from external & individual factors like differences in cultural values, beliefs, and morals that organizations are not supposed to address by using constructs to screen individuals at the time of hiring, offer onboarding, or continue training everyone to cultivate a broader understanding of the impact of practicing them actively. It's more often left up to an individual to manage their unconscious biases, beliefs, thoughts, and blind spots. For efforts at the individual level to work, one needs to have adequate knowledge about the root of the problem, how to identify it, what to do about it, and how to approach it incrementally. Professionals often adopt one of the following micro strategies by cultivating different ways of thinking through situations.

- Looking at the problem differently (a favorite amongst Leaders, Managers, and Team Leaders)
    - 'Everyone manages problems differently. I need not handle it until it doesn't reach me.'
    - 'People are their own biggest enemies and not you. The time turns around for everyone.'
    - Convert it into an idle talk.
- Channeling your energy differently (a favorite amongst team members)
    - Is it worth spending your energy? Knowing which

problems are worth choosing to fight for saves one from a lot of drains automatically.
    - 99% of the problems are not problems worth your energy.
    - Expanding that 99% of energy in achieving your goals.
    - Convert it into a mundane talk.
- Get a mentor who has lived that life and understands your problem, is empathetic, action & result oriented, inspiring, motivating, and has easy energy to work through this while guiding you. (It is not a favorite as it is seldom available.)
- A handful of them opt to handle it with skills, build wisdom, and self-reflect to decide to change and do something about it with the help of organizational resources offered by the human resources function. (a favorite amongst professionals who have character strength, often are whistleblowers out of choice or subjected through their circumstances).

Does it help? For the most part, it seems yes, but actually, no. As the underlying approach is to brush off the situation at hand, which can promote the risk of being ignorant about any and everything. Eventually, organizations who care less and teams or leaders who choose to unsee what's seen suffer from a continuous cycle of recruiting new substandard professionals due to their existing professionals not wanting to sustain the malpractice of 'going with the flow and not knowing what else to do.'. Organizations frequently show much openness to address such issues deeply but often result in doing less in reality. They succumb to reasons of lacking enough power to get it done or contained by possible legal proceedings or lacking in prioritizing over executing business objectives. At the same time, not accepting that this single most important aspect of work culture can save companies the hardship of recurring and never-ending cycles of recruiting, i.e., sustaining well-groomed skilled professionals within the organization, self-motivated individuals delivering more than anticipated outcomes well, driving customer value, contributing to the company's longer-term vision, and helping keep the company's brand in the leader's segment amongst industry rankings.

The idea here is not to expect professionals to be perfect in their behaviors. The idea is to minimize the actively known practices of following unpleasant behaviors, actively bringing the malpractices to the forefront, acknowledging them, and staying on course to work through them on a day-to-day basis, and keeping room for empathy & understanding what it takes to be a human at work. So, we collectively contribute and build a culture everyone likes (loves) to return to and breathe in!

Skills are essential for professionals to develop so that their dreams live adequately. It need not be an arduous, tiresome, imposing, or boring thing to pursue. But it can become a daily fun game if one understands the impact it creates when practiced incrementally and persistently. It builds one's competence over time, and in the long run, it can also influence one's dreams to shape them up further.

Practice time. Let's get to it!

1. Individuals
    a. Identify the functional skills required for your day job.
    b. Identify the other skills that you currently practice.
    c. Identify the other skills that you would like to practice (at least one and at most three) with the level of mastery you'd like to achieve based on the contextual application of the same in your work.
    d. Identify the good behaviors you actively follow.
    e. Identify the unpleasant behaviors you inadvertently follow.
    f. Incorporate the above-identified skills into your plan to practice them in your daily work life.

2. Leaders, Managers, Team Leaders
    a. Get past one's biases by reviewing the checklist mentioned in the section for Individuals.
    b. Remind team members of their health resources & benefits and how & when to use them actively.
    c. Keep vigilance within the team to encourage good behaviors and acknowledge them.
    d. Get trained to keep vigilance within a team to identify and address unpleasant behaviors, acknowledge them empathetically, and offer to help through them. Create a safe space for teams to feel comfortable to open up gently about such episodes.
    e. Act as a liaison to find the right mentor to create additional support.

3. Organizations
    a. Consider introducing adequate mentorship programs for behaviors valued by the organization.
    b. Consider introducing mandatory, cyclic training programs bi-yearly, self-paced, and in-person for Individuals and Leaders. Training could include intangible skills building (from the list

discussed in this chapter), practicing nonviolent communication, handling unconscious biases, managing microaggressions, identifying your blind spots, effectively working through them, reporting incidents & seeking help, knowing the hierarchy structure within the organization for adequate escalations, knowing resources available to make use of, managing your beliefs & cultivating behaviors.

c. Model powerful, autonomous, non-bureaucratic, less lengthy & simplified processes to address reported incidences of unpleasant behaviors. Have three levels of stakeholders involved in the process immediately as any incident is reported. Most of the time, leaders are unaware of the problems that their teams are facing. They would greatly contribute to streamlining incidents by bringing a welcoming, open-minded, objective, and empathetic approach to managing reports.

d. Accept that work culture is the backbone of having a well-functioning workforce and focusing simply on the bottom line numbers will adversely affect work culture. Ensure all business functions, leaders, managers, team leads, and goals are onboard to incorporate this fact in reality. They support teams to focus on the impact and performance rather than just business numbers.

e. Start communities and digital group channels for the workforce to express and share their concerns and experiences anonymously.

f. Actively build a Mental Health & Well-being community for Mental & Emotional Wellness supported and funded by leadership at the top tier of the organization.

g. Provide adequate health resources for employees as part of the joining package and encourage them to know their benefits and how & when to use them actively.

CHAPTER 7

Values for Character

*'Everything that can be counted doesn't always count,
and that which can't be counted often counts for more.'*

- Albert Einstein, German-born American Theoretical Physicist

The world is a culmination of various opportunities that allow us to experience things that teach and grow us. As everything is temporary concerning our experiences, i.e., our sorrows, happiness, excitement, desires, memories, etc., one can wonder what stays with us through life.

It's the cultivated character based on individual values.

We are all on the path to developing and integrating those values through our daily practices and knowledge. While embedding them in our foundational nature is a lifelong process, how we do it differs in our adopted individual approaches. For example, many of us let life experiences grow within us, and many approach it as an intentional act of actively developing them. No method is right or wrong. They have their pros and cons. Some can help you to stay fluid, while others can help you stay flexible &

adaptable. Some can help you be objective, and some can help you experience ease. Any approach is good as long as it's positively working on you & the environment around you. At the same time, personal challenges keep you from actively practicing and staying true to developing values. For example, lack of will & motivation, lack of opportunities, lack of observation power, lack of following self-reflective practices, lack of problem-solving abilities, or a lack of understanding why this needs your time and efforts.

Much research done by renowned psychologists across the globe, through centuries, has identified that values are the core of our human existence, our connected nature of reality, and an effectively functioning unit of communities. Seeking a connection through our shared values is a human need. That is how communities are formed, sharing common values and goals. Working together gives us all a sense of harmonious, meaningful, and pleasant experiences. In life, if humans practice specific values actively and genuinely, they showcase higher levels of achieving satisfaction throughout their lives. Also, the more the practiced values are in one's kitty, the better the chances of receiving opportunities as one progresses in their mid-executive level career path. Optimally functioning & vested organizations or teams that fulfill their vision are, therefore, most benefited in the long-term when professionals are supported in actively practicing these values. It builds their character, which is required as a foundation for driving meaning in the personal & professional space they are part of.

Power of Values

When I decided to put forward my resignation at work, this was my fourth job, so I knew the pre-exit drill of pursuing a professional to continue working with the organization. It was one of those times when you know too much about persuasion, and then it loses its effect, value & novelty, enabling you to see right through. But this time, I was up for something new. The Senior Director of the business group chose to meet with me, and what happened next was something I didn't anticipate. He showcased the group's plans, and in the process, he showed me plans for new offices, team expansions, customer engagements, etc. He made genuine efforts to run me through the scenes of exciting work opportunities lying ahead. By willingly spending this time, he must have been saving a seat in his team, but how I thought of it was that

- 'He genuinely wanted me to be part of the team.'
- 'He values my contribution.'
- 'He saw something that 99% of my colleagues could not.'
- 'He expressed that I am needed.'
- 'He is my well-wisher.'
- 'He got me thinking!'

That's the power of humility, integrity, authenticity, and genuinity. It makes one and all feel that they belong! It's an art worth developing. As simple as it can get, if you get over your false ego and stay truthful to your conscience, then this is achievable. By one example of someone being themselves, I was inspired for life to be this person, to mirror these values, and to be this way. No matter how hard the times get or how high the stakes are, being a person of positive value always pays off. Because we are working in a world full of humans who value good character for developing mutually beneficial connections and pleasant experiences.

> *'The final forming of a person's character lies in their own hands.'*
>
> *- Anne Frank, German-born Jewish Diarist*

There are many values that one can adopt and exhibit positively. Here is a list of values essential for professionals to cultivate.

Authenticity

It's about being comfortable in your skin. It's hard to find productive grounds with individuals who they are not, so working together poses many day-to-day challenges of maintaining approachability, trust, etc. Especially managers, leaders, and team members with these traits are more successful, objectively focused & fun to work with. Authenticity is rarely encountered, as it requires anyone to understand themselves deeply, overcome their deepest fears, and embrace & accept themselves fully with their vulnerabilities to get their best selves at work.

Commitment, Determination, Grit

These values vary greatly by minor differentiation.

Still, to keep things simple, they represent one's ability to stay on course, follow it through, and persist through any difficulties encountered on the way, time and again. It's these values that converge together to build resilience eventually.

Honesty

One may think that honesty is subjective; when everyone has their version of truth, where is the place for honesty? Staying true to the time, place, and circumstances to the best of your knowledge & ability is showcasing honesty. Keeping one's conscience clear and humbly admitting to any blind spots, i.e., keeping one's mind open to learn information or facts that one would not otherwise, is humility. What you know today is a function of what you didn't know at some point. Keeping things in the perspective of the current circumstances without the intention of gaining any undue advantage is what honesty entails. For example, sometimes, all the details of an undertaken task, goal, or mission cannot be shared widely. Does one share partial information and leave it there? Is that honesty? Maybe not. Then how can one exercise honesty in such a situation? A simple exercise of humble, clear, assertive, open communication can save the day, i.e., with the right tone and enough clarity of message that some information remains confidential at this point and can be shared with a broader audience at an appropriate time, without being intentionally withholding information so that one can assert any type of power, authority, or manipulation over others. If one shares information partially without openness or enough clarity of message, it appears to be purposely hidden. Which invariably generates anxiety and triggers mistrust. It's easy to work through this and prepare in advance if you are vigilant enough to anticipate prior situations and red flags. Yes, many think that spontaneity and oversharing are authentic honesty. Well, It's not! Very few individuals get this right; spontaneity is a by-product of practicing honesty repeatedly. Practicing honesty intentionally can be daunting for some, but preparation can help one get in the right frame of mind before the action. Preparing a few statements, talking them out loud to oneself or in front of the mirror, and improvising can help. This might sound bizarre, but this works until it becomes one's second nature to practice honesty.

Humility

Humility is being indifferent to recognition of any kind, resulting in an inflated & unrealistic sense of ego, which doesn't mean rejecting recognition or not accepting rewards or acknowledgment. It means knowing and accepting that the results are the culmination of interdependent efforts and not independent efforts. This can be challenging for many as one can naturally not factor in upfront or behind-the-scenes support one receives to reach an outcome. Showing interest in everyone's benefit with an attitude of serving others and being part of the journey together makes the practice of humility much easier. Beyond the differentiation based on any title, role, qualification, position, power, abilities, skills, etc., lies the world of collaboration made easy with people exercising more humility.

Integrity

Practice of honesty and constantly working through cultivating values for the better while staying true to them in the moment without blaming others is integrity. For example, doing what you say and saying what you do, especially when no one is watching, showcases integrity.

Reliability

Being present, being available, doing what you say, and getting things done the right way all collectively exhibit reliability. Most importantly, lessening the gap between communicated and translated actions (despite anticipated results) brings a sense of reliability to individuals and their environment. This promotes teamwork, collaboration, and new opportunities.

Resilience

Resilience is the ability to get back up and keep going with a positive attitude to reach your goals as effectively as possible despite repeatedly encountering failures. Resilience with problem-solving ability can make anyone sail through the toughest and most unique challenges.

Respect

It is given that the most basic respect towards our individuality must be practiced in professional environments. This is a non-negotiable value. As human beings, we all come together and choose to spend our resources, time & energy with each other, creating something of impact for the world. If respect, as essential as it is, is lacking, then the foundation of any team, group, organization, or personal life is at risk. How can respect be exercised? It starts with verbal practice, largely what dwells within the heart and reflects through speech. There could be obstacles to practicing giving respect when someone does not possess much strength of a character, has had grave differences of opinions with or unpleasant past experiences, and many more reasons become obstacles latching onto one's false ego. But the reality is that everyone is admired, liked, and appreciated by someone. Our experiences with any individual are subjective; what is suitable for one turns out to be bad for another. Such obstacles are nothing but an opportunity to reflect deep within ourselves and see what it is within ourselves that is stopping us from giving/receiving basic respect to/from others in any situation.

We must take this chance every time we have access to it because we wouldn't want to be stuck in the vicious cycle of 'everyone wants it, but no one wants to give it.'.

Trust

Trust is a function of long-term engagement. But one must start any engagement with trust. Then, there are higher chances that the relationship becomes authentic, open, and harmonious than the other way around. That is, to build a relationship and wait for the trust to emerge one day out of nowhere. There are challenges with the practice of trust, and they are more significant. Entirely trusting anyone can subject oneself to another's manipulation and deceit, their trust being utilized unduly, and being exposed to the risk of their efforts going unaccounted for. One can take such experiences with a perspective that 'Well, if it had to happen, earlier the better.'. One is placed better if one figures out what works for the relationship and how to make amends in a situation of despair or rigid disagreements. Exercising a reasonable amount of trust can be a good start during the initial stages of working with a team. If needed, then accounting to build and keep healthy professional boundaries can help relieve some of the struggles as one further works along. But approaching every encounter with less baggage of the past, exercising willingness to give it a fresh new attempt, being present, and being helpful to others doesn't go unnoticed, which increases one's reliability and can help build trust.

Values for Character

List of Values

Accountability	Equality	Job security	Risk taking
Achievement	Ethics	Joy	Safety
Adaptability	Excellence	Justice	Security
Adventure	Fairness	Kindness	Self-discipline
Altruism	Faith	Knowledge	Self-expression
Ambition	Family	Leadership	Self-respect
Authenticity	Financial Stability	Learning	Serenity
Balance	Forgiveness	Legacy	Service
Beauty	Freedom	Leisure	Simplicity
Being the best	Friendship	Love	Spirituality
Belonging	Fun	Loyalty	Sportsmanship
Career	Future generations	Making a difference	Stewardship
Collaboration	Generosity	Nature	Success
Commitment	Giving back	Openness	Teamwork
Community	Grace	Optimism	Time
Compassion	Gratitude	Order	Tradition
Competence	Growth	Parenting	Travel
Confidence	Harmony	Patience	Trust
Connection	Heath	Patriotism	Truth
Contentment	Home	Peace	Understanding
Contribution	Honesty	Perseverance	Uniqueness
Cooperation	Hope	Personal fulfillment	Usefulness
Courage	Humility	Power	Vision
Creativity	Humor	Pride	Vulnerability
Curiosity	Inclusion	Recognition	Wealth
Dignity	Independence	Reliability	Well-being
Diversity	Initiative	Resourcefulness	Wholeheartedness
Environment	Integrity	Respect	Wisdom
Efficiency	Intuition	Responsibility	Working hard

Table List of Values. Not an exhaustive list.

It's easy to speak about the values and know their benefits; the difficulty lies in keeping the motivation and willingness to pursue and practice them in the real world. The success of well-exhibited values can also become a function of our surroundings, beliefs, life experiences from growing up years, etc. It takes a lifetime to build these values. Having said that, can everyone cultivate all of these values? Although we all have the capacity to build values, transform & evolve ourselves, at the same time, we must acknowledge that all of us have a predisposed nature from birth, and we showcase natural strengths and growth areas accordingly. Therefore, everyone must be mindful that cultivating some values could come across as easy for one individual but be difficult for another. Another question stands: is it viable to work on them? Yes, it is possible, keeping an open mind that every step guarantees incremental progress, being self-observant & introspective, and deeply acknowledging the subtle but priceless rewards it carries for a long time in our lives & the world around us. Every successful endeavor of an individual or an organization choosing to cultivate positive values enjoys longevity in a conflict-free working environment and a healthy work culture that effectively encourages openness, ease, genuineness, learning, and collaboration. While the outcomes of developing a character based on positive values are promising, there are things to anticipate and prepare for when one practices them.

1. Identify what drives you to keep building on your values. How do those drivers relate to your purpose? Clarifying why you are pursuing this endeavor helps you stay on course in the long run.

2. Taking the first step is a mammoth task. But once you set yourself into an action-oriented mindset and question everything that takes your attention. Like for any situation, question the action you undertake.
    a. Does taking action make sense?
    b. Does taking no action make sense?
    c. At what pace does taking action make sense?

   These questions do the initial groundwork for anyone to get started. For most of us, rewarding oneself at the end of an action works its magic on continuing our motivation to proceed. Set a target, split it into bite-sized actionable tasks, and attach a reward system that keeps you yearning more upon completing each task. Also, an accountability partner can help with setting yourself into action mode. Group or community activities are a great example of moving the needle forward while inspiring each other to stay until the finish line. Be more creative and keep clocking your progress forward, pause and check what worked for you or others, and experiment with it. The key is to keep moving with anticipation and observe that something novel emerges from the experience and process.

3. It's a popular myth that only inherently passionate individuals can make it to the finish line. It's not just about passion but clarity of thinking, persistence, determination, resilience, and willingness to dabble in new and uncharted territory with self-belief and trusting your abilities to make it to the end. That's the goal to achieve. Keeping the purpose as one's target in mind, everything achieved through the process is a by-product. This mindset of growth helps immensely to keep looking and never settling.

4. Be open to being criticized, ridiculed, rejected, ignored, disregarded, i.e., any negative reaction which, when thrown at you, hits your solar plexus & shakes your self-belief a bit, if not more. The idea is to develop a model to manage such feelings well in advance. Preparation is the key! Once you have prepared your mind for one of the worst possible outcomes, rehearsed anticipation works through it. Acceptance in real time of such behavior keeps you still in an objective mindset rather than triggering your irrational brain to act & reject any new experiences coming your way. Criticism will always be a part of the game as one tries new things to build values. Criticism is also valuable if we look at it objectively; if not immediately, then keeping an introspective hour aside to dive deep and reflect on what is needed to change regardless of how others are behaving. Keeping yourself in check

with integrity and honesty shall ensure that you stay on the path to working on your values. Reminding yourself that this endeavor is your most precious gift to yourself. Making yourself vulnerable in front of the world out there will not be an easy path to traverse. But being vulnerable is what it takes to be human; the rest live a life of fear. So when your intuition kicks in through those gut crunching & heart sinking feelings, set the stage to surpass that fear. Once through, you know how to rinse and repeat. What matters is choosing to play the game of life by showing courage & bravery and coming out in the arena to live. Eventually, you will come out as a winner with a great character, bringing deep meaning to your life and life around you!

5. Save yourself from the trap of reasoning, 'It's their fault.'. Fault-finding, blame-shifting, or finger-pointing at others is tempting when one lacks the capacity to self-reflect, mind their lane, and humbly accept to be open to change. It comes almost instantly and naturally to us when confronted with our shortcomings; after all, it threatens our identity. To surpass this is like climbing Mount Everest at 100 miles an hour speed. No matter the truth, in every situation, there is something you can learn for yourself. Keeping this objective mindset is not easy to practice at the moment; only if we knew how we could address this one thing well! The solution starts as explained here.
    a. Cultivate a practice of daily self-reflection.
    b. Take a mental pause before justifying your actions and blaming others.
    c. In that mental pause, contemplating openly (as there is no one there to judge you other than yourself, and you should refrain from judging anyone, including yourself!). This is your open space; keep it free of judgments.
        i. Strip out all the negative tones, words, gestures, and sounds attached to the negative reactions thrown at you.
        ii. What is the conveyed message? Write it down!

    iii. Find a point of feedback where you need to improve yourself.

    iv. Accept that the reactions of others are unfortunate events that happened and have passed by. It doesn't define you completely. You can choose to keep it to yourself or throw away the parts that will not help you move forward positively on your goal. You can live with it, staying in the past. Because they choose to stay in their ways, you are presented with this opportunity to experience your improvement. Being thankful for this chance can help shift your focus from the moment to reality.

    v. Imagine the same episode happening to you again, but you are improvising on the feedback received this time. Imagine a positive outcome from the situation.

d. Accept that your emotions are valid and acknowledge them deeply. Also, take a resolve to do something about it beyond the initial healthy expression of talking it through so that the feelings do not take over your rational thinking during any tough situation in the future.

e. Accept that no one is surpassing or subjugating you while you are working through this process. There is no hurry to get anywhere, and the only focus one needs is to contemplate and experience this event differently this time.

f. Accept that no one is watching you or your past mistakes. Go out there as if it's a new attempt at everything you do today. This fresh mindset will help ease the pressure created by unpleasant episodes and internal dialogues.

g. Understand that your circle of influence and control over it is within the boundary of your life and subjected to improvements you can make. Environments, surroundings, circumstances, time, situations, and

Values for Character

individuals; everything will come and go. The only things that will stay with you are your experiences, innately built values, and vision. In this process, keep yourself open to welcome anyone who likes to join hands harmoniously. As a result, you are progressing, growing, heaps, and bound more gracefully than ever!

6. Starting with your immediate surroundings, one value at a time can help. Showing small acts of kindness and observing yourself, asking,
    a. How does it make you feel?
    b. How are others around you receiving it?
    c. How are they benefiting from it?
    d. How are you benefiting from it?
    e. Do you want to improvise further the next time or keep going as it's working well?

These all can start with simply being present in the moment (explained further in the next point), engaging actively, keeping calm, and exhibiting values through actions. For example, make a genuine effort to ask someone you speak to at work or home, 'How are you doing? How is your day coming along?' Not just saying but with all intention to hear and genuinely engage with a well-replied response. You will be surprised to be genuinely interested in others rather than seeming interesting to others; how such small acts make your and others' day so pleasant. Keep creating smaller rituals to fit in the values you'd like to develop. Values like integrity, respect, reliability, trustworthiness, truthfulness, etc. Choose from the list of values provided in this chapter or add your own, which you think can help immediately and in the short-term at your workplace & in your personal life. Note differences in outcomes and keep at it, as it hardly takes any time off your schedule to practice them.

7. Having focus and attention in the moment one is working with. It'll enhance effectiveness through one's deep involvement in the process. Engaging oneself this way makes every task seem to be done efficiently, like being present in your relationships and

listening to your bodily & psycho-physical cues when you are happy or need much care. The power of your attention can spill its positive energy into everything you choose to do, and you end up doing it well.

8. Remember the impact you are trying to make for yourself, the world around you, and at large. Once you give your surroundings gifts of your pleasant character, reciprocation is guaranteed. Positive change within you and around is a matter of someone standing up and making a resolution to keep the moment as light, easy, kind, and honest as possible; in other words, don't take life too seriously; effective moderation is key, keep room for some light-hearted play (not ignorant). Everything around you brings a positive ripple effect, especially with this light energy.

Attitudes

When values can take a lifetime to build, what can help in the short run? Many face this question when cultivating values remains an arduous process. In the face of adversities,

- Where is the time to actively pursue character building?
- Where is the motivation when one struggles with working on their immediate goals, which helps them get a secure monthly paycheck?
- My skills and abilities will get me through the correct career progression; that is enough.

With all these questions comes a feeling of being tired, complacent, fearful, unexciting, and self-doubting. Our feelings about things we do affect the very thing we do. This means our feelings affect our actions, be it in a person's life like family, self, friends, relationships, job, career, failures, success, etc. Positive feelings drive productive actions, or simply whether we take action or not. One can say that I have no control over my feelings; they just flow within me. To a certain degree, our attitudes support the feelings we feel. That is the chain of effect; our attitudes determine our feelings, and our feelings determine the possibilities of our actions. Therefore, our attitudes contribute immensely to our success in any arena. For example, to eye the next leadership position, beyond skills and abilities, one must have attitudes of collaboration, decision-making, assertiveness, mindful risk-taking, etc.

The question is how to build good, positive, and well-functioning attitudes. What does it take to build them? They are a function of our belief system. For example, one can choose to believe that the world is not a safe place to be in. It may affect and influence some of my attitudes, feelings, and actions. Like, It can affect their decisions about traveling around the world or even commuting within a city block. For one to believe anything, it doesn't need to be true in reality. It can just be true for oneself. The good news is that beliefs can be cultivated with effort, even now. Beliefs can be shaped. Beliefs are shaped by our conditioning from the external and internal world within us, i.e., the environment we grew up in, our relationships, subject matters we feed & expose our minds to, affinity we feel towards specific environments, collectively we call our realities. That is why beliefs can vary from person to person, as can their attitudes, feelings, actions, and outcomes, as each is independent of the other. This is shown in the illustration, *Shaping Attitudes by Restructuring Beliefs*.

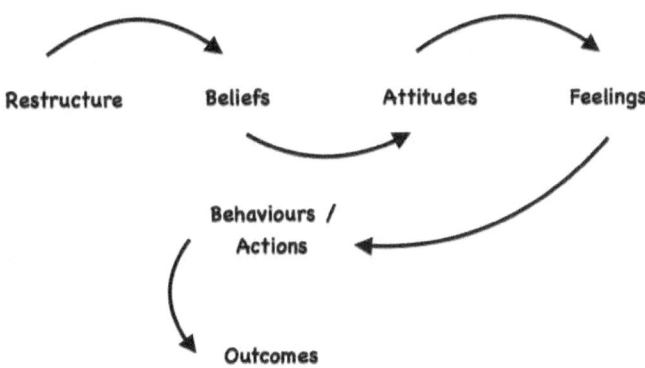

Shaping Attitudes by Restructuring Beliefs,
Inspired by the Origins of Our Belief Systems - Shad Helmsetter (1982)

So anyone can start with shaping their beliefs by resolving to change them, but it doesn't work like that. Shaping our old beliefs, which have strong imprints in our subconscious minds, can require one to go beyond feeding them with new information. In this case, 'I am taking a resolve.'. Being specific works. For example, 'I resolve to make every moment an opportunity to change my beliefs about the world being generally a safe place to travel around. With good precaution and safety measures, I can be equipped to handle any unforeseen situations…'. It's about what you frequently tell yourself about yourself or the world around you. Another example is if you keep telling yourself that this organization's work culture is bad for you, then you start believing that it is; putting blinders on anything positive that goes around you and failing to factor in any good will make you believe your initial thought. Having said that, not every organization, team, group, or individual's problem lies in carrying faulty beliefs. One must not hide or brush off every singular problem attributed to belief systems anyone carries. One needs to exercise a rationalized, objective mindset to understand, accept, and take appropriate accountability for where the root cause of any problems lies. As anyone's circle of influence lies with taking personal responsibility for shaping their own beliefs and how they are leading their thoughts about situations, it can make or break someone's progress in building a good attitude. Beyond personal responsibility, determination, zeal for fulfilling life, and willingness to change are key to even begin shaping beliefs in new ways.

There are so many things in life that we aspire to have, e.g., becoming more successful at anything, holding better self-belief, getting organized, planning travels, getting a well-paying job, executive positions, overcoming stress & anxiety, becoming a subject matter expert, stop worrying, becoming confident, experience better relationships, have more supportive environments, they can all be addressed by a simple functioning of what we feed our minds on a day to day basis. And with how many details. How we speak with ourselves from moment to moment. Over time, when your beliefs start to change, you may find that it affects your surroundings and your choices differently than before, e.g., some associations may fizzle away naturally as the previous belief systems hold lesser meaning in your lives; beforehand, knowing that treading an unknown path can be a difficult process to go through, can make you prepare to accept your realities with an open mind.

Attitudes are part of life, be it good or bad. Any attitude could be instigated by situations at the workplace, such as when an employee is not considered for promotion, is given bad feedback, or is treated badly & not supported or rewarded for their contribution to the team etc. All these can present opportunities to witness one's attitudes. Everyone can improve their attitude by making a simple and easy change in how they speak with themselves, within themselves. And this small thing can bear such good results. Starting with saying positive things about yourself can create ripple effects in your surroundings that can change the way you feel and can affect the actions & outcomes attached to them positively. It could be anything you'd like to improve, e.g.,

- Becoming confident.
- Successfully communicating.
- Having great interpersonal relationships.
- Taking high-stakes decisions.
- Achieving goals successfully.
- Becoming humble and authentic.
- Overcoming personal struggles.
- Building healthy self-beliefs.

Devising a detailed script for repeatedly training your subconscious mind with this new information can help cultivate different attitudes. For sample scripts, look for the free mobile app mentioned in the *Resources* section of *Chapter - Your Journey*.

You can also take some inspiration from the list here, some essential attitudes for professionals to cultivate.

1. Approach people with pleasantness and sternness whenever required.
2. Avoid fault-finding and blame-shifting. This doesn't serve anyone and creates the worst results for everyone involved.
3. Avoid lamenting. Instead, do something about it. And if you

cannot, save your energy by not speaking of it. Also, understanding the difference between healthy expression of oneself and lamenting can be the most critical knowledge one can have.
4. Choose to focus on the things at hand and give it the power of your full attention.
5. Cultivate empathy to consider others and their context.
6. Do what you say, say what you do.
7. Exercise the joy of giving without getting anything in return. Once a week, the 5-minute practice of selfless acts that do not have any direct or indirect outcome toward your promotion or professional image or any returns.
8. Keep your end of the bargain and own accountability.
9. Keep your vision, mission, and goals significant but your endeavors and actions small enough to enjoy the process.
10. Keep an enthusiasm about life.
11. Lead when no one else is raising their hand. Leadership can be built without a formal title, position, role, or permission. Raise your hand to do something within the boundary of your work but not directly related to it. Building skills that are not directly applied today and seemingly not valuable are the skills that come in handy when you need them later on. This can help cite more opportunities for growth & progression in one's profession.
12. Learn something new daily from books, work, people, mistakes, opportunities, or the environment around you. And log it.
13. Plan, get organized, and get things done. Action taken leads to an outcome.
14. Often, practice building something and giving to others.
15. Practice empathetic candor.
16. Practice harmonious give-take.
17. Practice self-compassion in the face of tough situations.
18. Practice courage to challenge status-quo when necessary.
19. Practice intrinsic motivation, which is not controlled by your

feelings or mood.

20. Practice lightheartedness. Understand this is not about going overboard or being ignorant; balance the scale of being fun and responsible simultaneously.
21. Practice taking perspective, questioning, and objective curiosity over keeping assumptions and making judgments.
22. Show up every day, every time, with your best self.
23. Showcase mutual respect through small acts like punctuality, responsiveness, attentiveness, and following through things.
24. Stay objectively curious and learn new creative ways of doing things. Practice objective curiosity; empty curiosity can prove dangerous to a false ego and keep you locked in a fake sense of being, having achievement, or being helpful.
25. Take more calculated risks.

Everyone likes to win; everyone wants to win. Winning through tangible, material outcomes is easy to come by when hard work and effort are put in. This measure of success soon wanes its winning trait when one understands that it takes more than mundane efforts to bring meaning to one's endeavors. Developing values and attitudes to bring meaningful success is a key skill for anyone who wants to live their dreams happily! It takes years of practice, patience, and honesty to keep working at it, but in the process, one receives unmatched zeal to live their dreams.

Practice time. Let's get to it!

1. Individuals, Teams
   a. Make a list
      i. Values and attitudes you possess, and you want to cultivate. Start with one or two in each area.
      ii. Devise your positive self-talk against attitudes you find yourself stuck with, and listen to it daily. Use the free mobile app mentioned in the *Resources* section of *Chapter - Your Journey*.
   b. List one practice for each value & attitude you'd introduce into your daily schedule plan.
   c. Practice them for at least 4 to 6 months.
   d. It's an iterative process of improvement. Take notes of the approach that worked, along with challenges and new micro strategies to adopt & solve them.
   e. Decide to reward yourself for making progress every month.

2. Organizations
   a. Define which values your culture duly represents.
   b. Define which values your culture needs to adopt.
   c. Define which attitudes you have due to the culture you recognize yourself as part of.
   d. Define which attitudes your culture needs to adopt.
   e. Define what aspects of each value and attitude the organization can help the workforce to work on.
   f. Define groups, resources, duration, and training to set up and monitor experiments before rolling out an organization-wide change of practices.

CHAPTER 8

Work-Life Balance

'Everything that exceeds the bounds of moderation has an unstable foundation.'

- Lucius Annaeus Seneca the Younger, Stoic Philosopher of Ancient Rome

The word 'Balance' throws most of us off our balance in many ways. Every one of us has lived a life full of struggles, happiness, challenges, celebrations, etc. Each of us must have already known that if there is anything that cannot be achieved at any given point in time, then it is an absolute balance. Be it a balance of any kind. Sadly, the concept of Work-life Balance speaks about the underlying issues rather than its benefits. The difficulty with achieving work-life balance is similar to that of

- Living in today's fast-moving or adopting ever-expanding arena of businesses.
- Being willing to create impact & value in the end consumer's life.
- Providing any kind of valued product or service offerings for an extended period.

We may think that today's era provides ample conveniences to achieve work-life balance quickly. While it is good to have conveniences at our fingertips, we must all ask whether these advancements and perceived value have created any value in our lives or taken away much from us.

- Whether it is saving time by using quick services on your mobile.
- Whether it is getting more done while using that saved time.
- Whether it is getting closer to your goals as a result of getting more done.
- Whether it is achieving tangible outcomes in one or more forms like money, status, or position.
- Whether it is making you happy or miserable.

Why do we often enforce and talk about work-life balance in the professional world? During a global pandemic in 2020, professionals suffered various forms of fatigue. Resulting from overconsumption of information, putting over-the-top hours at work, contracting the disease and jumping back to work after getting cured, overconsumption of digital content, and over-exposure to constant Electromagnetic Fields (EMFs) coming through devices and online connectivity, etc. Burnout and fatigue were evident as our minds are not designed to undergo continuous stimulation and overstimulation. Somehow, this proved more challenging than the daily rat race professionals often find themselves in. Such behaviors were also influenced by having extra time at hand to spend at work, other sources of outdoor entertainment were next to nil due to the longer duration of lockdown, and behaviors of individuals were induced by the fear of uncertainty, e.g., doing what they can do to manage uncertainty posed by economic changes, reducing the chances of potential job loss by putting in extra hours at work. Everyone has many compelling reasons to prioritize work over everything else, like self-regulation, health, downtime, rest, leisure time, relationships, etc.

Did we cause this burnout and fatigue ourselves? Or were we exposed to external and internal conditions that led to a widely recognized burnout in the global workforce? Partly both. Through the pandemic, we just found a reason to experience the same work-life balance dilemma together at the same time. We experience imbalances in work-life that we go through on our regular days. But now, sharing this worldwide phenomenon led us to speak about work-life balance on a global platform. Mental Health and Well-being concerns were raised during & immediately the period after to keep the workforce functioning at their optimal best. Collectively, these situations forced everyone to question themselves: what are their most important priorities, not just at work but personally? What did it entail to have a work-life balance? For lack of a better term, some called it work-life harmony, work-life blend, etc. One can name it anyhow; the questions we asked ourselves were right. We needed a global pandemic-like situation to align ourselves with new perspectives, plans, habits, and ways of functioning to practice *effective moderation in respective aspects of our lives*; that's what I refer to as Balance.

What work-life balance means for one can vary from another. But primarily, it could mean finding reasonable satisfaction out of your current professional and personal life events combined over a period of time. Achieving effective moderation and satisfaction can be subjective to every area of our lives and different for each individual. Everyone can define it simply as the percentage of time & energy spent in both broadly critical areas of their lives, i.e., personal & professional. No matter how you choose to think about it, there is a way to achieve work-life balance by following a set of frameworks. Here is one that delivers on understanding work-life balance as achieving *effective moderation in respective aspects of our lives*.

1. Start by defining what work-life balance means, especially for you. Write it down, visualize it, and experience living it.
2. Accept that work-life balance can be subjective and doesn't mean attaining perfection or mimicking the lives of others. It means identifying aspects of your life that matter to you and spending enough time to drive happiness from each aspect.
3. Ask what it will entail and assign a percentage of time and energy you would like it to have and are currently giving to. You can focus on high-level areas like personal care, health - body, mind, soul, relationships, work or job, finances, learning, entertainment, interests, or hobbies. Expand these areas to further sub-categories like interests, which may include traveling, reading, exercising,

sports, etc.
4. Take an honest look at the list you have prepared and see which struggles keep you from attaining a reasonable work-life balance.
5. Consider those as the goals you want to work towards.
6. Adjust your expectations while keeping some leeway, i.e., room for making further adjustments as you learn new things about yourself and your life.
7. Ask for reasons. Which aspect of reality stops you from living through rational circumstances or situations in each area?
8. Be truthful about what is in your control to change.
9. Accept what you cannot change and list what you can do to achieve your goal or make a change.
10. Prioritize the change you would like to work towards.
11. Define an accountability chart for yourself to follow through with the action and achieve your goal. You can start with a simple task tracking format containing task, day, time, duration planned, status, etc.

This starting model can help you see a clear picture of what work-life balance means in your context, identify what is helping or creating hindrances to achieving it, and where the opportunity is for you to take action towards it. Further, if one carries out this exercise every quarter, looping in their learning as they go along, it can help anyone:

- To gain perspective.
- To look at life more meaningfully.
- To have satisfaction, looking at the progress one is making towards their goals.
- To keep one honest about changing realities of life and prioritize one's plans as needed.
- To realign their expectations rationally early on to avoid disappointments much later, i.e., to only realize worthlessly spending their time & energy.
- To stay on course based on the new circumstances.
- To increase personal accountability toward making progress.

- To keep light-hearted enthusiasm alive.

This may seem like an intentional and systematic process, but how often do we pause and see what gifts we already carry? There is a dire need to be mindful of the gifts of blessings we hold in the form of support, opportunity, interests, capabilities, relationships, etc. Pausing to reflect on our goals & plans is becoming increasingly important when we surround ourselves with so many unhelpful distractions on a day-to-day basis. Work-life Balance neither needs to be a subject talked about in a seminar nor a subject to read in a blog post to soon forget about. It can translate into actual, rational, tangible, and meaningful outcomes in one's life.

What is life if it is not worth living?

And the worth of your life is in your control. You can take charge by creating this opportunity for yourself to attain effective moderation.

Practice time. Let's get to it!

1. Individuals
    a. Go through the questions mentioned in the chapter to define what work-life balance means to you. Identify the top three areas you would like to start working on.
    b. Three areas can be further segmented into durations based on anticipated outcomes, e.g., short-term, long-term, etc.
    c. Keep a weekly log of your progress and alter any details in the action plan if any course corrections are needed.
    d. Review the list quarterly to see the impact of achieving your short-term and mid-term goals.
    e. Write about your experience (preferably handwritten, on a piece of paper). Collect them in a jar to look at them further as you work through more goals. Revisit and re-read some of the experiences you've already gone through. That will keep things afresh and bring ease into your life.

2. Teams
    a. Go through the questions mentioned in the chapter with team members to define what work-life balance means to you as a team or a business group. Identify the top three areas you'd like to start working on.
    b. Three areas can be further segmented into durations based on anticipated outcomes, e.g., short-term, long-term, etc.
    c. Keep a weekly log of the team's progress and alter any details in the action plan if any course corrections are needed.
    d. Review quarterly with the team, assessing the impact of achieving short-term and mid-term goals.
    e. Write about the team's experience (preferably handwritten, on a piece of paper or sticky note). Collect them in a jar or create a sticky note board to look at them further as the team works through more goals. Occasionally revisit and re-read some of the experiences the team has gone through. That will keep things afresh and bring ease into the team dynamics.

3. Organizations
    a. Take active feedback about work-life balance practices from the workforce, industry & field and bi-yearly review any employee benefits, policies, and engagement activities that need revision.
    b. Defining an organization-wide work-life balance umbrella model can be challenging and ineffective. Therefore, giving autonomy to refine and adopt practices that work at business groups and team levels can help retain a good work-life balance.

CHAPTER 9

Culture of Diversity

'Your title makes you a manager. Your people make you a leader.'
- Debbie Biondolillo, Apple's former Head of Human Resources

What Debbie Biondolillo says is as true for Organizations as it is for Individuals.
Yes, read that quote again!

From equality to diversity, we all know these words of revolutionary thinking, movements, and trends. We have seen the effects of them being part of the work culture over generations. We have seen its impact on our lives and the world around us. The movement for equality started from aspects of race and gender but moved to so much more in the professional arena, such as equality of pay, respect, opportunity, etc. At many levels, riders of equality have made the world progressive, but when it comes to the capabilities based on gender, that is, men and women, it has not proved conducive. As we understand, the fundamentally different nature of these genders is designed to function optimally through time immemorial. At the risk of sounding stereotypical, the truth is gender equality has lived its purpose, and in the current age, it is a dead cause because of its loose narrative.

Respecting & accepting the unique existence & capabilities of different genders and what they bring to the table in the personal or professional arena is the thought to lead in the correct direction as that perspective is genuinely unbiased, individualistic yet community-centric, open-minded, and equity-driven rather than being rigidly equality-driven. The progress of generations is rooted in how humans have evolved through the years. Centuries since, society has celebrated, respected, and accepted the two predominant genders for their innate individuality. We have seen more harmonious growth, which contains meaningful success, supporting a win-win narrative to include all of them. A narrative that accommodates their strengths and integrates entire communities to build harmonious cultures, holding safe spaces for everyone to co-exist as their best selves (by and large). In the 21st century, the number of women stepping into the professional arena is increasing more than ever. During this time, the workforce is exposed to many work cultures that ride on simple equality-based factors, eventually facing many challenges. Women subjected to challenges and struggles in this age often hear voices saying, 'Woman, work it out!'. Many ask, 'But how?' and they are often answered as,

- By not challenging the status quo, keep yourself as a clone of what is widely accepted.
- By not speaking up so that you can contribute.
- By not asking for help, figure it out on your own! Saying, 'No one can help if you don't want to help yourself; charity begins at home.'.
- By accepting the behaviors that are not acceptable.
- By being a man! In matters of behaviors, personality, ambition, thinking, communications, adopting priority models & ways of doing things, etc.
- By changing your innate self. From being less feminine, i.e., affectionate, cheerful, compassionate, gentle, gullible, shy, soft-spoken, sympathetic, tender, and understanding, to exhibiting more masculine traits, i.e., aggressive, ambitious, competitive, decisive, forceful, independent, individualistic, leadership abilities, risk-taking, self-sufficient.
- By getting yourself together and acting strong.

- By being data and facts-driven, life will get perfect!
- By ignoring the effects of natural aging cycles on overall health, well-being, and priorities at hand.
- By keeping your life priorities aligned primarily with work.
- By finding a godfather or a godmother at work for promotion.
- By not keeping space to voice your concerns, by keeping it to yourself.
- By trusting colleagues who are untrustworthy in the name of teamwork and making friends at work in the name of team relationship building.
- ...

Interestingly, if you look at these, they are nothing but examples of the characteristics and behaviors exhibited by men at work (for the most part). Shows the expectation pattern that our systems are designed around exhibiting masculine personalities & behavior traits, and that's the gold standard for progress & success. Such deep-seated expectations, mindsets, and behaviors pose problems for keeping the stereotypes alive and not allowing the status quo to be challenged to see real, conducive progress. It creates a blockage to infusing diversity within the organization or allowing professionals to come to work as their best selves and not just unquestioningly emulating what is widely seen as progressive & acceptable behaviors at the workplace.

A lack of space to feel psychologically free and to be their authentic selves at work is a painstakingly real struggle. It is a more significant obstacle to driving the women workforce (or those who exhibit feminine traits at work) to join the corporate world, as they are often misunderstood for their expression of femininity. For instance, being vulnerable with their emotions and crying out their stress occasionally at work can be seen as a sign of weakness and unprofessional behavior. I know of many other women, including myself, who have been through this due to being misunderstood or ununderstood or not supported in the right way as the circumstances demanded or difference in how both genders process information & situations in the social context. The preceding judgments for expressing any vulnerability at work are 'This is not in anyone's best interest.'. But being supportive and understanding of such vulnerability shows that you accept and acknowledge professionals at work as humans who can exhibit occasional outbursts of emotions, which humans do! Understanding a woman's vulnerability gives her the undying motivation, grit, sincerity, commitment, creativity, determination, loyalty, and integrity to get through any challenge they face. That's a strength, not a weakness, as it is perceived through wider societal norms. Everyone, not just women, can feel emotions while showing feminine traits. They are an integral part of being human. But specifically for women, repeatedly encountered situations at work that drive these emotions out are when

- Their hard work is not acknowledged.
- Their mistakes are criticized, and they are not given constructive feedback.
- Their individuality is rejected & pushed over, naming it as gentle.
- They express their emotions; it's assumed they can be pushed over or walked over.
- Their due credit is passed on to fulfill someone else's dreams.
- Their core right-brain-centric strengths (EQ) are discounted over widely accepted left-brain-centric strengths (IQ).
- They are called in at the end of the queue to have a seat at the table or to lead.
- They are subjected to stay open to any misbehaviors without expecting any accountability or corrective action against the doers. Leaving them to handle disgust and grief caused by the loss of dignity by themselves alone.
- They ask for help, and it's assumed they lack the intellect or capabilities to do their job independently.
- They ask for support, and it's assumed to be needy behavior.
- They give more to others, and it's assumed to be an expected behavior or a pleasing attitude.
- They say the truth repeatedly, and it's assumed to be an act of dishonesty or some form of scheming.
- They achieved something with the help of others (as a team), and it's assumed that others do their work and they have no contribution

of their own or hold accountability.
- They stop asking for help, and it's assumed that they are either not confident & submissive or arrogant & prideful.
- They speak of any problem, and it's assumed to be solved by improving their communication & being assertive.
- They put themselves out there, and it's assumed to be aggressively opportunistic & competitive.
- They stand up for themselves, and it's assumed to be bossy & authoritarian.

These and in many more ways, we see women suffer silently (and shake off struggles) under the name of abiding by the majority protocol followed on the ground that is based on adopting masculine characteristics; no matter what they do, how they do it, with or without the individuals around them, they ought to face lower-end of the bargain, i.e., often their genuine & positive efforts are unnoticed, unrecognized, not considered, shamed, misinterpreted, and unduly judged. When I mention these, it represents a generalized view of actively noticed practices at an organization, a specific group, or a team level. Many simple things can be followed to work through foul practices, creating difficult environments for women to function productively. At large, professionals can adopt a mindset of paying attention to the healthy balance of their behaviors using masculine & feminine traits whenever necessary and actively try to work through any challenges on a day-to-day basis. The practice of being more empathetic, accepting, acknowledging, and welcoming than rejecting or overlooking makes it even more difficult to manage. We'll further discuss more practices throughout this chapter.

The new age movement of diversity expands the definition of gender equality even further by showing that not just gender but also race, religion, social background, etc., has a role in defining grounds of equality and maintaining diversity at every level. In recent years, the realm of diversity has further expanded into something called diversity, equity, inclusion & belonging, widely abbreviated as DEIB. What does DEIB mean?

Diversity

Having a workforce that culminates different genders, races, religions, ages, roles, positions, neurodiversity, perspectives & and thinking styles.

Inclusion

Having a workforce that feels included at the workplace through thoughts, behaviors, and actions practiced by professionals at all levels. Everyone being included could look like having their voice heard, their opinion counted for & acknowledged, their efforts received well, their contributions recognized & rewarded, they feel wanted by the organization & environment they function daily in, being & having a safe space to work & grow with, and acceptance of their best selves with their talents, skills, knowledge, and experiences.

Equity

Having adequate access to opportunities to use one's strengths and cultivate their growth areas, support for growth & feedback, and leaping beyond considering typical professional profiles for opportunities & promotions.

Belonging

Having a sense of belonging to get their best selves at work every day, in the most genuine way possible. Without being affected by the anticipation of negative behaviors causing roadblocks in their professional growth. A lot of good behaviors can be modeled by training, but the practice of genuinely putting in effort reflects a change in individuals inside out. That eventually reflects in one's daily dealings. They feel equally empowered to speak up and challenge the status quo without worrying about getting punished, commanded, or rejected by seemingly uncomfortable colleagues at every level. They feel a strong sense of support for doing the right thing, no matter the odds against it. They are positively worried about doing the right thing as they know that transformation at any scale happens with a change of perspective. They exhibit a sense of loyalty and a willful wish to continue working toward the company's mission & vision while at the same time working on their individual growth.

Much research exists to make professionals and organizations aware of the benefits of the DEIB movement. If implemented correctly, it can benefit everyone.

- The more diverse the workforce, the more innovative, creative, contributing, and happier work cultures become.
- Organizations can
    - Have a bigger talent pool across different functions, ready to expand themselves and explore different career paths through their tenure in the company.
    - Have increased positive employee engagement.
    - Have trust built at all levels, downwards, sideways, and upwards. Culminating in a culture of openness and honesty, eventually improving proper decision-making and overall performance.
    - Have an engaged and forthcoming workforce that drives quality business value delivered to customers.
    - Have meaningful success in attaining their vision.
- Individuals can
    - Show up as the best version of themselves.
    - Showcase more affinity to an organization, a group, or a team they work with.
    - Feel more connected with their environment as they feel a sense of belonging.
    - Hold less to no concerns about being assertive with colleagues at all organizational levels.
    - Feel confident about being their best and who they are as individuals, as the skills and value they bring do matter.
    - Empowered to take calculated risks and exercise their creativity to improve performance and impact.
    - Feel more empowered to use technological advancement and tools to voice their difficulties and contain proof of behaviors that are not required to be tolerated and hidden. Participating in building a

community where everyone flourishes by doing the right things and being at the receiving end of it.
- Have meaningful success in attaining their dreams.

With so many benefits, one can ask why DEIB is not a prevalent phenomenon practiced or exists evidently in every professional work culture. Firstly, we are just getting started with having relevant conversations. Secondly, there are cons of having too much diversity that can lead to more chaos than coherence as desired. Too little diversity can stifle an organization's, team's, or business group's ability to stay creative, innovative, genuine, relevant, and committed to a cause in the long run. Thirdly, as with everything good, it's harder to achieve in practice, and there are known barriers to it. These barriers are linked with realities of basic human existence, which are,

- Seeing non-conducive behaviors at work
    - Microaggressions.
    - Unconscious bias.
    - Bullying.
    - Unjust judgments.
    - Armed leadership driven by punishments & commands.
    - Changing one's behaviors unwillingly to what is accepted, e.g., by changing your innate self from being less feminine, which is affectionate, cheerful, compassionate, gentle, gullible, shy, soft-spoken, sympathetic, tender, and understanding, to be more masculine, which is aggressive, ambitious, competitive, decisive, forceful, independent, individualistic, leadership abilities, risk-taking, self-sufficient.
- Unilateral view of capabilities that culture practices should remain the same at all organization levels.
- Resisting that diversity is fact and inclusion is a choice.
- Cultural beliefs and values.

- Employee experience situations where there is a lack of respect and dignity that one deserves, for instance,
    - Struggles & humiliation of being named a diversity candidate.
    - Having to feel helpless & virtually supported for name sake while someone goes through
        - (Borderline) Sexual Harassment. Wondering if 'Being a Woman is a curse!', the '#MeToo!' movement is not a fad.
        - Name-calling.
        - Slandering.
        - Shaming, mocking.
        - Bullying.
        - Merely being used to grain marketing eyeballs and wondering, 'Why am I born a Woman? Am I a curse for one cause and a blessing for another?'.

Any barrier that requires solving the problem through changing human behavior is always deprioritized. It could be because of reasons such as

- Lack of will and acceptance to work through complexity.
- Lack of prioritization & ownership at an individual or organizational level.
- Excessive focus of the organization, group, or team on tangible business outcomes, bottom-line numbers, and lack of acceptance of the need to prioritize personal growth.
- Consistent time and resources are required to make it work reasonably well, keeping them from attaining tangible business outcomes.
- Lack of understanding, acceptance, and willingness that it can take a very different set of inclinations, sustenance of power, ideology, beliefs, values, and thinking patterns to be worked upon continuously.

Despite these prevalent issues, as DEIB has reached a stage of being a worldwide phenomenon due to its benefits, throughout the world, every organization is working through and putting efforts to prioritize & deliver whatever little benefits through DEIB initiatives. This work is not a standalone opportunity. The results are applied at the individual or organizational level. It's for both. It is an inclusive effort interconnected and interleaved in its inputs and outputs, i.e., who puts in the efforts and who gets the benefit of outcomes. Let's look at what organizations can do about their DEIB objectives and achieve those goals to make corporate work cultures more attractive than ever.

1. **Which Problems?**

   Generally faced problems by women in the workforce are also faced by any other minority & diverse workforce within an organization. So, it is of utmost importance to note and align the earlier discussed problem areas to your organization's DEIB goals. This can be a good starting point for organizations that want a quick start and do not have volunteers to participate in identifying objectives or goals for DEIB initiatives.

2. **Engagement at Every Level**

   A holistic approach can be conducive for organizations to adopt, where one can start from the top-tier professionals to set the movement in motion by setting the right priorities, infusing the middle-tier professionals in the process to lead, and driving the change through the bottom-tier professionals on the field. At the same time, making them part of curating the process of change based on their valuable inputs, suggestions, and routinely collected feedback. Please note that tier terminology simply reflects the workforce based on their responsibility structure rather than undermining or uplifting their position in any way.

   DEIB initiatives and processes can consider incorporating umbrella practices discussed here to increase workforce

Culture of Diversity

engagement.

a. Throughout my career, I have been fortunate to have worked with many men and women who have considered everyone for fair opportunities. Although they have been less than one percent of the workforce, that is the chance to find professionals who are vested in your success and helping to support or make way, who are empathetic enough to understand what you bring to the table in the professional realm. The fact is, you find all kinds of professionals everywhere. Still, the unempathetic leaders, managers, and team members who exist and brutally focus only on business outcomes outnumber the empathetic ones who understand and support the lot. It is then the responsibility of organizations to set the right priorities and foundation, empower leaders or managers to practice courage in saying 'Yes' & 'No' when appropriate, and not just focus on business outcomes or numbers but prioritize culture as their winning proposition.

b. Ensuring DEIB objectives are integrated with all practices and business units within the organization.

c. Actively applying the DEIB lens to everything a company does, e.g., hiring, training, businesses, product or service deliveries, and customer engagements.

d. Starting to facilitate difficult conversations can also be one of the initial steps organizations can consider. A third-party vendor or community-based organization can be consulted to facilitate the required focus, attention, and intentional action to start the creation of in-house safe spaces for open conversations. Educating the workforce about using technological advancements as probes can give the right tools to execute these strategies at the workplace without making it a nightmare for employees to participate and keep their comforts vested.

e. Leadership commitment, a vested stake in the process, and mandatory buy-in are the keys that need to be in place before commencing this journey.

f. Drawing adequate attention to the capabilities and will of leaders & stakeholders to ride on their DEIB goals.
g. Integrating volunteering & DEIB and not keeping them isolated. This can help make inclusivity more accessible across organizations and amongst different units, teams & individuals.
h. Impact for everyone at every level can also be achieved through the involvement of an entry-to-mid-level workforce. Ripple effects of having starter conversations can help manage microaggression and unconscious biases at work & personal space. Eventually, positive behaviors will be expanded to communities, society, and the world by having conducive policies in place. Acceptance from the top leadership of diverse individuals, skills, and their contributions can be the key to creating a culture of safe spaces at all levels. This can help integrate DEIB within work cultures.
i. Appropriate accountability to make outcomes transparent and assigning the proper priority to DEIB efforts can help keep up the momentum to make progress together.
j. Outsourcing accountability, i.e., by incorporating third-party community-based consultations, which will come up with regulated checks and balances, keep the company accountable to not just rely on the organization's group for accountability and leave room for bureaucratic practices to be obstacles for truly being DEIB.
k. Invite customers or clients to be part of the collective DEIB efforts by making them aware of DEIB-infused engagement practices.

3. **Holding the Right Conversations**
    DEIB conversations can be of various kinds with various stakeholders of organization units, focusing on

a. Understanding the company mission, vision, objectives, goals, priorities, and reasons to operate with them effectively. Thereby defining what DEIB means to the organization as a whole and at the level of a business group, unit, or team.
b. Enlisting
   i. Leadership motivations.
   ii. Employee needs.
   iii. Gaps in employee experiences.
   iv. Organization goals, worldwide brand standing, and address the gap between market image and employee demands.
c. Identifying a pool of employees that you can advocate for some of these issues, start having conversations, and partner with employees who are passionate about these topics.
d. Conducting awareness events about the formation & availability of employee resource groups, taking leadership buy-in, and budgeting to spread it out and wide within an organization.

4. **Talent Acquisition**
Tailor the talent acquisition strategies, starting from creating more inclusive job descriptions, adopting the language that potential candidates would understand, expanding reach and marketing, e.g., different job roles can be published for college recruitments, referrals, and cultivating skills.

5. **Curating appropriate Brand**
Showing up as a brand to attract diverse talent. For example, making orientation videos and job descriptions listing the successful candidate profiles and skills required.

6. **Opportunities for Promotions**

   Creating equitable spaces means having opportunities available for all, with adequate support for resources & growth. Having to put mindful and intentional action to formulate the process of being promoted, spreading the knowledge, giving support & opportunities for execution, and following through it.

7. **Training**

   To promote conducive behaviors and make the environment more receptive, respectful, and fun, training must be made compulsory, delivered in person, and enforced for all employees. Training to manage microaggressions, unconscious biases, bullying, armed leadership, sexual harassment, creating safe spaces within teams, etc. Conducting such training in person and making it mandatory is the first step in increasing the chances of being practiced in day-to-day reality and engaging everyone at once beyond their individual interests. For example, agnostic of gender, a left-brain-centric workforce may often resort to shrugging off ideas of creating safe spaces for many reasons, such as they may think it's beneath them and useless to spend time cultivating such interpersonal behavioral traits, they may hardly want to exercise courage and accept their lack of empathy & deal with it, etc., not understanding that through safe spaces and an open mind, everyone can be more receptive to ideas of embracing feminine and masculine traits as the situation demands and respecting each other for what they bring to the table. Through this, it increases effective collaboration, promotes the exchange of ideas & infuses creativity and a sense of camaraderie.

8. **Policies**

   Tailoring Policies that are conducive to DEIB adoption, like usage of appropriate language for communication, e.g., tones, expressions, choice of words, etc., setting protocols of seeing through rules & regulations while keeping behaviors in check, and supporting the workforce with the right helplines and skilled team to work through problems when they arise.

9. **Infusing DEIB at All levels**

    Creating safe spaces for exercising empathy. Drive training and knowledge sessions to build workforce understanding so they can know how they show up empathetically with their contribution towards products, services, interactions, and policies they deliver. Also, showing that they are supported to unlearn and relearn ways of handling issues at the workplace can make them comfortable & open about trying it.

10. **Prepare for the Stand-still**

    Foresee previously discussed challenge areas upfront that can cause DEIB efforts to stagnate or eventually stall, such as
    a. Buy-in from leadership and alignment to their motivations.
    b. Not beginning the journey.
    c. Resistance to change at the employee level.

'Culture eats strategy for breakfast.'

- Peter Drucker, Austrian-American Management Consultant, Educator, and Author

In addition to the subject discussed here, the culture of diversity can have many more viewpoints, perspectives, and guidelines. But this is the starting point for individuals, teams, leaders, managers, and organizations alike to come together and make sure they collectively build a work culture by embracing diversity & inclusion, practicing equity, and having a place they belong to contribute. For individuals and organizations to have their visions pursued with the best efforts, culture is the key to unlocking those opportunities on a daily basis. So let's make all our efforts count and not just focus on business strategy but give culture a chance to evolve.

Practice time. Let's get to it!

Keeping up with the idea that building and maintaining work culture is part of everyone's responsibility, this section deliberately keeps the guidance available for all to consume in their capacities, i.e., individuals, teams, leaders, managers, or organizations.

1. Identify one of the aspects listed above which can be incorporated in your organization as part of the DEIB initiative.
2. Identify leadership team members and stakeholders vested in DEIB culture infusion for their active support, policy alignments, funding, and exercising appropriate prioritization.
3. Raise your hand to volunteer or build a community and work with the DEIB initiative group within your organization. A space to start the right conversations and curate training, spread awareness, and curate programs that can help infuse DEIB culture within your group, team, and organization as a whole.
4. Recommend and/or engage third-party DEIB consultants, coaches, or organized companies who can help keep DEIB efforts ongoing and raise adequate accountability to meet your DEIB goals.

PART IV

Being the Dream!

> *'There is only one corner of the universe you can be certain of improving, and that's your own self.'*
>
> *- Aldous Huxley, English Writer and Philosopher*

Our most significant obstacle to reaching our highest potential is what sits within us. Our deepest selves! Changing ourselves to evolve into a higher consciousness can be daunting for most of us. But this is essential for knowing what our true selves want to communicate to us, what it means, and how we can leverage that to attain our full potential.

Accepting that, the process of discovering your true self and realizing your full potential will entail pain, discomfort, and struggles. The fact that one goes through pain is a reflection of their growth. For example, you build bodily muscles while lifting weight at the expense of momentary pain. Without pain, there is no change in our respective situations; without change, there is no transformation of our realities; without transformation, there is no hope for evolving our consciousness; without higher consciousness, there is no scope for being dream-ready; and without being dream-ready, there is no experience of joy and happiness for a long time.

Our most essential goodness is born out of pain.

Being the Dream is to find yourself, seek the truth, and not settle for less. Such self-discovery is for the bravest but is the only path to meaningful success, evolution, excellence, and true joy, which can present us with feelings of free spirit, courage, and knowing our core identities.

What does it entail to be the dream?

CHAPTER 10

Not just Intellect

'Everything that irritates us about others can lead us to an understanding of ourselves.'

- Carl Gustav Jung, Swiss Psychiatrist and Psychoanalyst

My new world, in a new city, I transitioned into a new company. With a role that I had earlier experience working on, but the nuances changed. I was an expert on a line of software products to provide specialized consulting services to the customer. I acted as a liaison between the customer and the products team to improve the product offerings based on market demands. The job required high levels of intellect, deep technical knowledge of the product line, processes of delivery systems, functional knowledge of the customer's industry domain, and customer-facing engagement skills. The new role was a breath of fresh air in the midst of my life in a different city, team, and work dynamics. At the same time, as with any new endeavor, it was challenging because of the fear of the unknown or unfamiliarity. The culture of Silicon Valley-based companies is very different; it is egalitarian for most parts and encourages autonomy. I was getting used to interleaving and learning about new teams, functions, and roles, which mattered to putting my best performance forward and helping customers achieve their goals. Because the project engagements were short-duration, I had a chance to work with many different teams and explore working relationships with more colleagues at work. Despite difficulties adjusting to newness, I was optimistic about getting by my days to reach my yearly professional goal. It proved to be seemingly easy at the outset but overwhelmingly difficult internally. The outlook of a few individuals around me at the workplace started to affect my productivity and peace of mind, which often resulted in chaos, borderline shaming, and bullying. I tried changing my physical environment, often focusing on the work at hand, cultivating a positive attitude, and looking forward to keeping my eyes on bringing value to the customer's goals that I was pursuing.

A day came when all of this that I was absorbing and holding back within me came together as a breakdown! I was taken aback by many individuals constantly slandering me with statements that had no relevance to my work and had no incidence or action to precede the reason. It was all done in a manner without having any remorse about being ruthless to someone. I did not choose to retaliate; instead, as I always preferred, I started focusing internally on what transpired to get me to this stage of unrest within myself. I was feeling the deepest sadness, rejection, disrespect, and isolation in the environment that I was working in. It affected my motivation a lot, and so did the quality & outcome of my work. I felt unwelcome. This was not acceptable to me, but having no adequate guidance to get through this, I finally decided to reach out to the organization's Human Resources (HR) team. I raised my concerns regarding the team's working environment and sought guidance about how it could be addressed, as I neither had any authority nor prior knowledge of working through such arid challenges. I was shocked and taken aback by what I heard next; the only guidance shared with me was,

'If you can't help yourself, then no one will!'

I felt further rejected. I couldn't make anything of this statement; all I did was reach out to a professional who was an expert in the field, knowledgeable, and had the power to hold up accountability, seeking help on subjects I had neither exposure nor working knowledge of. On the one hand, this seemed like asking me to get on with things as they are! On the other hand, it seemed that they chose to avoid the accountability of the situation at hand. Stating something unhelpful at the moment left me feeling like I was standing alone and getting to where I was, suppressing my emotions, having no space for expression or productive collaboration, and being exposed to continuous unnecessary judgments. I felt hopeless with the world around me, thinking if the HR function promotes such practice, how far will I progress to solve the problem at hand? After feeling discouraged by not receiving any constructive help or support, I had no option but to take it upon myself to stay true to my personal accountability and carry on my work engagements with greater difficulties every day. Every day, struggling to keep myself detached from the unnecessary drama, power struggles, backhanded appreciation, slandering, and egocentric team members made me realize that I had to create some distance mentally (if I can't maintain a physical distance as I had no option but to work in a team setup.). That was the best I could do then: shrugging away the problem caused by my environment and continuing to prioritize only work, which seemingly affected the company's bottom line more. This was farther from the truth, as my immediate work environment affected my work output's pace, interest, quality, and sense of belonging. And so it does for anyone subjected to such situations!

A few years later, I came across Daniel Goleman's book *Emotional Intelligence*. Now, I could combine two and two. I understood that what I went through during the situation showcased a lack of Emotional Intelligence in practice. Rather than having empathy towards one, what was chosen then was a malpractice of unhealthy management of personal accountability. That day, I realized the HR personnel was telling me there was no room for support, no room for resolving such issues, no room for being human at the workplace, 'Woman, work it out on your own.'. In hindsight, this experience made me more positively independent, self-reliant, self-assured, and looking inward more often than others. This is when my journey of intentionally building emotional intelligence skills, specifically within the professional arena, as a woman, started. It was not a subject matter of being and acting sexist or feminist in any way; it was about me starting to understand the challenges that are faced by professionals, women in particular, because of their naturally different constitutional orientations and because their strengths are widely perceived as weaknesses (refer to the discussion from *Chapter - Culture of Diversity*). I chose not to select resentment of any kind and started exploring what could work to solve such situations in the future.

Thinking deeply, we all know that to carry out any daily function, we need balanced functioning on both sides of our brains: the left brain (logical, learning, rational) and the right brain (emotional, creative, expressive, social), which are responsible for doing different things greatly together in unison. They are so effectively interleaved that the outcomes are seen seamlessly and spontaneously in our behaviors and actions. In the professional arena, for most job functions, one could assume that your day job is mostly concerned with using your intellectual capabilities, i.e., handling information, being logical, and making rational decisions based on facts, data, and perceived knowledge. But a lesser-known fact that is not paid much attention to is the practice of our emotional capabilities, which is a culmination of building, refining, and using our intelligence. Intelligence itself is a subtle subject matter which, to a layperson's understanding, may look like showing healthy tolerance towards ill behaviors of others, understanding others' feelings before one can act, being socially apt, and regulating emotional expression inwardly & outwardly. Basically, being a practicing empathetic human! A skill essential for cultivating healthy, productive, effective, and harmonious relationships. Beyond our intellect, this skill, which is the most essential of all, is our emotional intelligence.

Emotional Intelligence is a key skill for any human interaction, considering the longevity and benefits it offers individuals. Work cultures with more practicing empathetic professionals showcase many skills (listed below) during their day-to-day functioning, which also spill over into their personal lives.

Personality Skills
- Empathy

- Change Tolerance
- Trust
- Stress Tolerance
- Flexibility
- Emotional State Management

Life Skills
- Time Management
- Decision Making
- Assertiveness
- Accountability
- Social Skills

Professional Skills
- Communication Skills
- Presentation Skills
- Collaboration Skills
- Customer Orientation Skills
- Innovation Skills
- Leadership Skills

These skills shape one's personality as they become progressively part of one's identities. But more often, we find organizations talking about it and providing information to understand the subject of emotional intelligence. But lacking focus and ensuring that information turns into practically executable guidance, it just doesn't remain a subject matter of talking; everyone walks the talk, keeping hand-in-hand together. When it comes to putting in work, what to work towards can be easily understood from the emotional intelligence skills model, which focuses on what it takes to build emotional intelligence and what it entails, inspired by the book *Emotional Intelligence 2.0* by Travis Bradberry & Jean Greaves, that is,

When Personal Competence = Self-Awareness and Self-Management
While Social Competence = Social Awareness and Relationship Management

Developing emotional quotient (EQ) is a function of building our competence. Competence at a level that requires working in personal and social aspects integrated but can be worked independently. Some micro-strategies that can help cultivate each aspect of building emotional intelligence & increase one's EQ are discussed below.

1. Self-Awareness through Self-Exploration & Self-Discovery
    a. Assess reasons why unpleasant reactions transpired for you, internally and/or externally.
        i. Is it coming from a violation of your personal values or beliefs?
        ii. Is it coming from any acquired unconscious behaviors or actions?
        iii. Can you find other situations elsewhere where you can relate these emotions?
        iv. Get a neutral perspective from an outsider.
    b. Avoid rating your feelings as good, bad, or worse. Accept them as they are. Let them be!
    c. Be observant of the consequences of your emotions.
    d. Be comfortable with being uncomfortable.
    e. Identify your emotions, i.e., feel, notice physical changes, and name them.
    f. Identify red flags, i.e., what is causing discomfort?
    g. Let the discomfort not overrule your mood; stay focused on the present. Take note of what reactions are transpiring, internally and/or externally.
    h. Make a persona of yourself when you are experiencing stress. What do you look like? How does it feel inside? How do you behave? What happens to you and others? What transpired as a result of stress? Are there any internal or external dialogues you practice when in stress? What are your go-to actions or strategies to cope with stress? What is working and not working, and what are the reasons why they are working or not?

List things you can change, starting from your values, beliefs, behaviors, attitudes, and actions. Rehearse how will you make that change next time. Record the outcome of real situations.
i. Take a zoomed-out view of yourself.

2. Self-Management
   a. Accept that change doesn't happen instantaneously but progressively. Your daily practices of self-awareness & self-management are meant to go through an incremental change rather than leading towards perfection. Not giving up on this endeavor can be the single most prominent rider to bring success.
   b. Create a vision board to see what your success entails in front of your eyes daily.
   c. Cultivate a micro-learning attitude, i.e., learning from every smallest of encounters.
   d. Divert your focus on something else for a moment, like feeling the texture of your clothes or breathing deeply (Box Breathing or Sama Vritti Pranayama technique). Especially when unpleasant emotions are experienced.
   e. Find humor in the situation (reflecting on the subject matter or realities, understanding the difference between humor, mocking, and insults).
   f. Get organized, and keep your surrounding space clean, clear, and open.
   g. Get support through personal growth coaching.
   h. Have long-term goals, make them known to others, and seek support to fulfill them. And never give up on supporting others or seeking support from others when necessary.
   i. Ignore it for the moment. Come back to it when you sit with it doing self-exploration.

j. Know when you need rest, rejuvenation, or a break. Get yourself at a harmonious pace by practicing mindfulness techniques.
   k. Learn something new every day by practicing problem-solving techniques.
   l. List down any life aspects where you have the right to freedom without being dragged by any dogmas. Remind yourself of them often, daily.
   m. Observe and regulate your internal talk.
   n. Practice anticipation of unpleasant situations.
   o. Practice downtime with things that bring you joy.
   p. Record identified emotions, red flags, and behaviors.
   q. Regularly practice breathing techniques to reduce stress in the moment and cultivate natural bodily tolerance for emotional strength.
   r. Take the support of a community or a neutral individual who is not vested in the situation as much as you are.

3. Social Awareness
   a. Anticipate social engagements by planning in advance, i.e., scheduling, time commitment, learning cultural nuances to engage better, keeping room for flexibility, and staying committed.
   b. Learn how to practice understanding others' perspectives better and learn about the situational context.
   c. Observe self & others by observing body language and verbal communication tonalities, listen attentively, learn to take the pulse of the situation accurately, be adaptable, and be present.
   d. Practice being present with anyone, doing anything.

4. Relationship Management

a. Be flexible and open to listening to new viewpoints.
b. Be more interested than act interesting.
c. Be there when you say you will be. Build trust by small acts of kindness practiced daily with everyone around. Keep expectations and outcomes at bay through the process while citing & taking more opportunities for self-reflection.
d. Keep yourself approachable by often letting others know of your available support.
e. Learn and adapt to different communication styles. Explore and see what works best in a situation. Bring your best to the situation as it demands.
f. Learn how to communicate feedback to others and receive feedback from others. Feedback that is constructive, direct, with maximum clarity of intentions, and with an appropriate tone of delivery. Start with understanding the difference between feedback and criticism.
g. Make an appropriate connection by calling and remembering others by their names. Make it a point to deliberately remember one or two strikingly good things about everyone you meet.
h. Practice saying it out loud and often acknowledging others, providing context for any misbehavior, apologizing when required, welcoming others to be their best selves, stating your intent genuinely, and keeping your ego in check. Remember, you have nothing to prove or earn by staying captive to your biggest enemy, I.e., your ego; lean beyond blame & understand or ask what is there to fix here.
i. Stay curious (mostly objective, not necessarily always).

Over and above, these practices can help anyone to develop better EQ with a set of overarching skills, such as,

- Staying true to oneself, inwardly and outwardly.
- Knowing that learning is a part of success & failure, learning is a continual process, not an event.
- Noticing, experiencing, and accepting the results of cultivating emotional intelligence. Having trust in the process to work itself out for the best outcomes; stay fluid.

One may often find heavy struggles on this path of developing emotional intelligence and emotional strength. For the sake of simplifying the discussion, categorizing the larger workforce's gender identity as of a man or woman, one may wonder who gets affected by these struggles more. Although both men & women are subjected to behaviors lacking in emotional quotient. But in the patriarchal cultures of the world, this is by far experienced more by women. The solution is to develop empathy & understanding of what others may go through, to introduce effective responsibility & accountability models to adhere to and to keep egocentricity in check by increasing trust-building activities & forming professional camaraderie. To support these, one must also understand some of the characteristics exhibiting emotional immaturity in practice, how exposed one feels in the situation, and the characteristics exhibiting emotional maturity.

- Behaviors and attitudes commonly exhibiting emotional immaturity:
    - Low empathy struggles to put themselves in others' shoes. Or practicing cognitive empathy, i.e., ingenuine practice of empathetic behavior, a deliberate thought process to gain undue control over others through deceit.
    - The ability to change is less.
    - Immaturity with the functioning language of an adult.
    - Self-referential, ego-centric, but poor self-reflection.
    - Rigid ideals, analytical thinking, driven by left brain activity, dwelling in either black or white.
    - Defensively oriented.
    - Everything is about them, all the time, every time.

- How does the one exposed to emotional immaturity feel?
    - Lack of motivation to mirror empathy.
    - Lack of grasp to see the person with their situation as a whole.
    - Lack of emotional or psychological safety.
- Behaviors and attitudes commonly exhibiting emotional maturity:
    - Self-reflecting.
    - Taking responsibility.
    - Holding accountability objectively.
    - Practicing behavioral empathy for others, which is thoughtful and genuine.
    - Recognizing others have a world of their own, too.
    - Showcasing good emotional connection, vitality, humor, and relating to others with authenticity or genuineness.

In reality, some men and women practice emotional intelligence when required by situations and benefit from their EQ reserves effectively. That makes only a few of them stand out, actively developing themselves and practicing these skills, while most struggle and give up, most likely early. The difference in motivation and continuity lies in their capacity to cultivate emotional strength. That's a function of how rooted one is within one's deepest self, i.e., practicing self-awareness through self-discovery. What is the strength of the connection they feel with themselves? That's the realm of compassion, knowing, feeling, acknowledging, accepting, working through, and being there for others to support. I.e., not just sympathetically understanding, not just empathetically putting oneself in other's shoes, but while being empathetic, extending oneself to be part of the solution & offer help-support. Compassion trumps empathy.

Build EQ, Start here.

1. The first step is to make your emotions your allies, not enemies. By being open to exploring the self-awareness practices discussed earlier.

2. Having knowledge and awareness of some (not an exhaustive list) of the reasons for resisting the practice of EQ at workplaces,

   Men often think that expressing EQ behaviors may result in the following aspects.
   - Affect them losing their command and power.
   - Affecting their assertiveness negatively.
   - Fear of rejection.
   - Losing their power over their masculinity.
   - Not knowing how to balance masculine and feminine characteristics within them.
   - Optimizing their time, they would rather choose to spend it achieving goals and tangible rewards.

   Women often hold back from exhibiting EQ behaviors because of the following aspects.
   - The fear of not being taken seriously and sidelined.
   - The fear of not being accepted by being misjudged, shamed, bullied, mocked, or rejected.
   - Being taken undue advantage of their efforts.
   - The fear of being punished.
   - Being left behind in the race to achieve tangible outcomes.
   - Not being considered for opportunities.

3. **Step Zero**

   If self-awareness is step one in the process of developing EQ, removing motivation blockers for pursuing self-awareness is Step Zero, i.e., easing the struggle of handling those initial emotions that are obstacles to pursuing self-awareness.

   When you stop struggling with your emotions, they work for you rather than against you. Having specific emotions and getting that bodily feeling does not define who you are as a person completely.

Comfortably, sitting with your emotions is where it all begins. The process of working through step zero is mentioned below to simplify this beginning for you.

a. In any situation, understand which emotions you go through.
b. Name those emotions, e.g., happy, valued, excited, insecure, sad, anxious, lonely, tensed, thankful, appreciated, refreshed, peaceful, inspired, amazed, encouraged, hopeful, empowered, confident, engaged, curious, friendly, sympathetic, etc. Naming them makes them clear to your mind and body and makes a memory of what is happening. Use the 'How do we feel' free mobile app to practice this. Look for it in the *Resources* section of *Chapter - Your Journey*. Below is the illustrated table for *Labeling & Understanding Emotions. Scaling energy and pleasantness through Emotions*. It is an example of a list of emotions and how they affect our energy levels and give us feelings of pleasantness.

High Energy	Enraged	Panicked	Stressed	Jittery	Shocked	Surprised	Upbeat	Festive	Exhilarated	Ecstatic
	Livid	Furious	Frustrated	Tense	Stunned	Hyper	Cheerful	Motivated	Inspired	Elated
	Fuming	Frightened	Angry	Nervous	Restless	Energized	Lively	Excited	Optimistic	Enthusiastic
	Anxious	Apprehensive	Worried	Irritated	Annoyed	Pleased	Focused	Happy	Proud	Thrilled
	Repulsed	Troubled	Concerned	Uneasy	Peeved	Pleasant	Joyful	Hopeful	Playful	Blissful
Low Energy	Disgusted	Glum	Disappointed	Down	Apathetic	At Ease	Easygoing	Content	Loving	Fulfilled
	Pessimistic	Morose	Discouraged	Sad	Bored	Calm	Secure	Satisfied	Grateful	Touched
	Alienated	Miserable	Lonely	Disheartened	Tired	Relaxed	Chill	Restful	Blessed	Balanced
	Despondent	Depressed	Sullen	Exhausted	Fatigued	Mellow	Thoughtful	Peaceful	Comfortable	Carefree
	Despairing	Hopeless	Desolate	Spent	Drained	Sleepy	Complacent	Tranquil	Cozy	Serene
	Low Pleasantness					**High Pleasantness**				

Labelling & Understanding Emotions. Scaling energy and pleasantness through Emotions. From Permission To Feel by Dr. Marc Brackett (2019)

c. Do not fight or shrug the emotion off, and do other activities. Practice self-compassion for whichever emotions are felt.
d. Sit with it quietly and see where in your body you feel the emotion is active.
e. Once you gain that knowledge, you feel calmer within; repeat it until you are steady.
f. Ask yourself to identify

       i. What caused that emotion within you?

      ii. What can you do about it at the moment?

     iii. What can you do about it to rectify the situation?

To increase your competence, take cues from the list of micro-strategies discussed earlier in self-awareness and self-management.

g. Assess the gravity or strength of that emotion over you. What stage is it at?

       i. Stage 1: Is it proving to be an obstacle or challenge?

      ii. Stage 2: Are you feeling stuck?

     iii. Stage 3: Are you burned out?

     iv. Stage 4: Are you feeling paralyzed?

This shall help you identify what level of help you need, from yourself or reaching out to others. Keep in mind that there is no one-size-fits-all here. For stages 1 and 2, self-help and self-regulation by feeling your emotions and objectively working through solutions over four months to six months can help you gain some progress. For stages 3 and 4, get professional help from a coach or a healthcare practitioner to resolve deep-seated issues.

h. Respect your energy while at it! Masculine or feminine characteristics are all part of humans, agnostic of our genders. These characteristic traits need to be accepted, acknowledged, and celebrated rather than being suppressed, condemned, or rejected through some social dogmas. This openness can help everyone break the stereotypes of typecasting behaviors to genders. For example, dogmas like more masculine traits are exhibited at the workplace to drive success and good results. In that case, more feminine traits hinder the focus on generating outcomes at work or inducing self-disbelief by exercising soft skills. Embracing both characteristic traits, based on time, place, and circumstances, can give a chance to build more collaborative and community-driven work environments. This can pivot our thinking and actions by

i. Embracing inclusion, trust, & harmony by starting an individual journey of developing EQ.
ii. Growing beyond norms that impose more struggles & isolation.
iii. Openly accepting childlike enthusiasms, excitement with purpose, passion with grace, self-esteem, and overconfidence.
iv. Positively embracing one's journey of developing EQ. For example, one can share their success stories of developing EQ with the wider community at work and in the field.

As one's immediate professional environment is increasingly becoming a prevalent reason for professionals to leave an organization, other reasons being professional dissatisfaction with their immediate managers in line of reporting, lack of opportunities, lack of values alignment with the organization, lack of long-term career goals alignment, lack of transparency with high bureaucracies. This can be alleviated by prioritizing building more empathetic professional cultures that every individual and organization must actively pursue. This can eventually help sustain professionals as valuable assets and realize their dream visions.

Practice time. Let's get to it!

1. Individuals
    a. Taking personal accountability for identifying and working through each aspect of EQ. Prioritize two items in each aspect to start practicing for at least 4 to 6 months. Track results & changes and note them in a tracking sheet as a history log. Review the quarterly log to refine and rework items where you are doing well or introduce new ones for practice.
        i. Self-Awareness
        ii. Self-Management
        iii. Social Awareness
        iv. Relationship management
        v. Emotional Strength (Step Zero)
    b. Actively participating and cultivating personal & social competence models offered at team & organization levels.
    c. Building integrity.
    d. Broadening your outlook for the welfare of everyone involved and actively participating in sharing constructive suggestions for improvement.
    e. Once a week, practice building emotional strength by gaining more awareness of your emotions.
    f. Openly acknowledge the EQ behaviors of others for welcoming, promoting, and infusing the practice of developing EQ.

2. Teams
    a. Conducting in-person EQ training and workshops at a team or business unit level every quarter, not limiting them to leaders or managers but extending them to all team members, teams, groups, and group leads.
    b. Keeping EQ suggestion box for each team.
    c. Assigning designated EQ champions within a team to raise awareness and integrate efforts seamlessly.
    d. Organizing monthly EQ hours and sharing gratitude towards

each other through sharing stories.
   e. Acknowledging & rewarding EQ behaviors for welcoming, promoting, and infusing the practice of developing EQ.

3. Organizations
   a. Cultivating support systems in the form of communities and giving them adequate funding, autonomy, and authority to function and make a difference.
   b. Conducting bi-yearly in-person EQ training and workshops at organization levels.
   c. Organizing monthly EQ hours and sharing gratitude towards each other through sharing stories.
   d. Acknowledging & rewarding EQ behaviors for welcoming, promoting, and infusing the practice of developing EQ.

CHAPTER 11

Uncovering the Truth!

'Who looks outside dreams, who looks inside, awakes.'

- Carl Gustav Jung, Swiss Psychiatrist and Psychoanalyst

Again and again, how unsettling it was! I had my mind repeatedly wandering to find perfectly matching words to describe my present experience, feelings, emotions, and the world around me. I felt settled after finding this one; my nagging mind stopped here.

'Empty!'
That's the word. But knowing it, did I feel settled now?
It was not about the word; it was about my reality.

I was empty!

The feeling of emptiness consumed me in strange ways: achieving my goals but not entirely, being present but not entirely, feeling emotions but not entirely, expressing myself but not entirely, living life but not entirely, being alive but not entirely. Everything seemed in order, but at the same time, not entirely. Everything seemed to be perfectly perfect (to my notion).

Everything seemed to be going well, but at the same time, it was not.

It was indeed the lowest low that I ever experienced. I felt lost and disconnected. But I could not figure out what this was all about. I chose to introspect for hours, days, and months together but was not led anywhere this time! One of the days, it all came crashing down on my health. This was my signal that all my internal explorations were not working out, and there was something I seriously needed to attend to. Not finding anything in particular wrong through a formal health diagnosis left me with no hope. But also with no sign of concern, which was strangely odd. I felt numb, without having the will to move in life. I stopped. Since childhood, I enjoyed my solitude, so I knew this time it was not it. For the first time, I learned what it meant to feel lonely despite being surrounded by the crowd. With my little leftover interest in problem-solving for my disconnected self, I picked up on learning human psychology and became my first-ever client!

Out of nowhere that day, a book caught my slight attention. It was *Bhagavad-gītā As It Is by His Divine Grace A.C. Bhaktivedanta Swami Prabhupāda*, a concise handbook for understanding the purpose and goal of human life. This book has been lying in my library for years, but it never came to me to take it up for reading. Today, I naturally gravitated towards reading it. Not understanding why this one and why now? I stopped thinking further and attributed it to my influence of the spiritual home where I grew up in India. I thought of my grandparents & parents, how they influenced me then, and courtesy spiritual practices followed at home; maybe now those things are nudging me with this subtle curiosity to understand the endeavors of my grandparents. How did they live such a happy & successful life? However, back then, I followed what I was told without knowing what I was doing. I thought I was inclined in some faith, but it was primarily outcome-based and fear-based. Years later, after my graduation, I came to be agnostic of practicing spirituality for the longest time. Until this day! I wasn't sure what was in store for me through this book. But I had an innate feeling that this was what I was seeking. That slight curiosity reignited my eternal optimism & hope, which led me to read the entire book for three weeks straight. This was my fastest, nonstop reading ever. I was startled at what just happened.

The Sanskrit texts of the book were so rich and nectarine that I would not stop.

BG 18.63
iti te jñānam ākhyātaṁ
guhyād guhya-taraṁ mayā
vimṛśyaitad aśeṣeṇa
yathecchasi tathā kuru

English Translation:
Thus I have explained to you knowledge that is still more confidential. Deliberate on this fully, and then do what you wish to do.

Verse 18, Text 63 with English Translation from the Book Bhagavad-gītā As It Is by His Divine Grace A.C. Bhaktivedanta Swami Prabhupāda

At the rear end of the book, he had me at this verse! It felt like someone understood me deeply; someone was genuinely gentle, compassionate, and considerate towards me; someone willingly shared the most beneficial knowledge with me without preconditions and yet respected my dignity to exercise my free will to pursue it. It was an exhibition of a truly powerful demeanor by the speaker of the verse, Lord Krishna.

Through this moment, I found what was lost! My answer for feeling emptiness was in my lost spiritual connection!

I thought this was the one book to rule them all! How much time did I lose reading others until I reached this one? It was worth every word and every verse. A gold mine of wisdom, the wisdom of human life. A guide to living a meaningful, satisfying, and successfully happy life. I knew something was changing within me daily as I read through it. But reading wasn't enough as it is for most self-help books. This one deserved to be understood not from my limited perspective but from the original author's perspective. And my journey of true spirituality started then. Whenever I understood a verse from a qualified spiritual mentor, it compelled me to change my perspectives and fundamentally reach my core to change my beliefs, outlook, practices, and way of life. It's a journey, and I am still on it. But it answered my struggling questions:

- Who am I?

- What is my true purpose in life?
- Where am I going?
- What does my ultimate goal look like?
- Can I reach there?
- How can I get there?
- What is the right thing to do?

After trying multiple streams of yoga and various disciplines of spirituality for as long as a decade, what worked for me this time was the simplest and the most straightforward approach of yoga to attain one's spiritual goals, i.e., the devotional practice of spirituality called Bhakti Yoga. If practiced well, its benefits are seen on multiple levels: physically, mentally, emotionally, and spiritually.

- On a physical level, it can help manage worry, stress, and anxiety to promote overall well-being. The rhythmic chanting and singing in bhakti-yoga can soothe the nervous system and promote feelings of inner peace.
- On a mental level, it helps individuals navigate life struggles with grace and resilience. This way of life and belief system provides practitioners with eternal faith & trust in their abilities, a sense of inner strength and peace, enabling individuals to face difficulties with courage and serenity.
- It provides a path for emotional healing and transformation. This process helps individuals overcome negative emotions like envy, lust, anger, ego, pride, arrogance, greed, fears, and mental disturbances. Replacing them with positive qualities such as forgiveness, gratitude, and contentment infuses joy, bliss, peace, fulfillment, and knowledge.
- On a spiritual level, it helps to purify the mind & heart and cultivate qualities such as love, compassion, and humility. It helps foster a deeper understanding of one's true self.

By willingly & incrementally adopting the essential spiritual practices suggested in bhakti-yoga (from a total of nine), namely rhythmic chanting, meditating, reading & hearing texts of wisdom, clean habits for eating & lifestyle, etc. I could start observing differences in how well I was informed about what I was doing, going through, and choosing to do through my life course. This process is very different from any intellectually bound methodical approach. It is based on the concept of Love, Service, and Surrender, i.e., starting with how open you are to surrender your rigidity and preconceived thoughts and giving a chance to explore this new perspective on life and graduate into offering your life efforts in the divine loving service. This process gave me an opportunity to understand the difference between living life as it comes versus being intentional about it & functioning in your total capacity. Finding my true purpose, holding my purpose as a north star, and moving through obstacles while loving myself as I am. Accepting myself deeply and being compassionate towards my existence and that of others. It was like finding myself in a completely different way and healing inside out, very subtly. I would truly start learning and understanding the meaning of the Self!

One can question, how can I know whether I need spirituality? Or what do I need in life at any given point in time? Or how can I know what I don't know yet? To answer these, *Maslow's Hierarchy of Needs* can help put things in perspective. As individuals, we all strive to fulfill our lives as a culmination of many aspects through various stages. Through this model, one can begin to comprehend and lay out their direct or indirect needs and find obstacles to achieving those. The illustration below *Dr. A. H. Maslow's Hierarchy of Needs* shows all the levels in the hierarchy, with the bottom-most containing the most basic survival needs and moving upwards to more deeply held needs of human life to attain fulfillment and happiness.

Dr. A. H. Maslow's Hierarchy of Needs, illustration by SimplyPsychology

Many times, what comes in the way of addressing these needs is our core beliefs and values. Modern-day psychology offers many psychotherapy modalities to address our core beliefs affecting our values, value systems, attitudes, feelings, and thoughts. They also help us work through deep-seated impressions of unpleasant experiences etched in our subconscious. In today's age, any kind of healing is accessible to everyone. The only prerequisite to making it available is to be aware of your needs and goals to a certain degree, followed by knowing where to seek help to achieve them. With the advent of the internet, booming startup ecosystem, and social media, these services are made readily available to the masses to benefit from. These services act as supplementary to aiding one's approachability to spirituality. Spirituality and its practices make our personal growth, improvement, and success much more easily integrated into our daily lives. Making our body, mind & soul connection part of the solution to a fulfilling life.

We go through everyday life as the wind passes by without attentively accounting for where our time and energies are spent. These hectic daily life experiences perplex us by subtly consuming our deepest spirits and encountering questions like

- Everyone gets it, but not me.
- I am a failure.

- I am going to be stuck where I am.
- I am not a good person.
- I don't have it in me! I am not good enough for it.
- I have no option but to be bad.
- I won't be able to achieve it.
- It's too tough; I won't make it through.
- Never try thinking of negative outcomes. Staying stuck.
- Others won't approve of it.
- Others won't accept me.
- There are no opportunities for my progress.
- Why is it happening to me?
- I must…
- I should…

These seemingly negative statements could be understood as our beliefs about ourselves, others, and the world around us. These are rooted in one's self-doubt, self-disbelief, lack of self-esteem, and lack of acceptance of self and the world around us. These are widely known, but, in reality, they are challenging to overcome and demanding to cultivate a positive mindset. Why so? This is because many things we go through are ingrained in our behaviors and day-to-day functioning as human beings from our predisposed fundamental nature, upbringing, surrounding environments, education, relationships, cultures, etc. We hardly make the right distinction between whether there is something deep within us that needs our attention and work. We seldom seek out different perspectives, we seldom have time to be attentive to ourselves, we seldom have the will to be self-reflective, we seldom come out of shame that is imposed on us, we seldom dare to help ourselves against the societal dogmas attached to care for our mental & emotional well-being, and we seldom lack a right attitude to pursue what needs to be, i.e., having patience, showing perseverance, and caring enough about our deepest truest self to come alive.

Why do we rarely care about such subject matters?

Because we, as human beings, are naturally built to resist. Resist change and dwell in comfort and pleasant experiences, finding solace in what is already known to us rather than exploring the unknown about us in new ways. Changing our current realities may mean exposing ourselves to potentially encountering unhappy, struggleful challenges that may last longer than we anticipate. As creatures seeking success, meaning, and happiness, we often choose not to empower ourselves. Empowerment with the right information gives us hope to take a leap of faith, transform by taking action on it, and pursue the action through time so we see our real evolution. Changing our values, morals, and beliefs that have been part of us since our growing years can be threatening and feel seemingly unnecessary to make significant progress while living on the material plane of life. Those who do succeed in achieving this are truly living their lives! By living their lives, they live & breathe the dreams they set out to achieve without getting negatively consumed by them, i.e., being free from unhealthy attachment to endeavors and outcomes.

How can one Start this Process of Evolution?

The first is to cultivate a seeking heart and curious mind. The journey must commence with self-discovery and gaining self-knowledge while simultaneously managing our daily life course. We often find ourselves seeking external acceptance in difficult situations while choosing to protect our innate selves. Forgetting the very fact that every one of us is inherently loved & accepted and possesses uniqueness by default. There is no need to fight, resist, or prove it by seeking external validation and being stuck in unhealthy codependency. What we need is a healthy interconnection and interdependence. Through self-discovery and self-knowledge, one can remind oneself of one's innate being, make peace with one's inner self, truly accept one's uniqueness and that of others, and start seeing things from the right perspective. Answering these domains of questions and finding the right answers is a path to identifying your True Self.

- Self-discovery entails finding our misaligned motives & purpose deeply connected with body, mind, and spirit.
    1. Who am I?
    2. How do I identify myself?
    3. What is my real constitutional position?
    4. What is my understanding of life?
    5. Why am I here?
    6. What is my true purpose in life?
    7. What is the mission of human life?
    8. Why am I experiencing what I do?
    9. Where am I going?
    10. What does my ultimate goal look like?
    11. What do I deserve?
    12. What is the right place to be?
    13. Can I get there?
    14. How can I get there?
    15. What is the right thing to do?
    16. Why is there so much pain, struggles, and misery in the world while there is also happiness?
    17. How do I want to contribute to the world through this life?

- Self-knowledge entailing reflecting upon yourself
    1. What are my motivations and aspirations?
    2. What are my beliefs about myself, others, and the world?
    3. What are my morals and values?
    4. What are my insecurities & fears?
    5. What keeps me happy, and why does it keep me that way?
    6. What keeps me stuck?
    7. What do I like about myself, others, and the world around me?
    8. What do I dislike about myself, others, and the world

around me?
9. What emotions am I feeling at a given moment?
10. What is causing me to feel those emotions?
11. Why am I choosing to carry emotions I feel?
12. What do they mean to me, others, and the world around me?
13. Do I need to change their course?
14. How do I practice feeling emotions deeply?
15. What experience and knowledge do those emotions offer me?
16. Being guided by that knowledge, Why, What, & How do I need to make any positive change in my life?

How does it all fit in my Work-life?

Below are some aspects crucial to success in personal and professional endeavors that are cultivated through discovering, understanding, and managing ourselves. They are developed along with the longer-term practice of spirituality to build our Spiritual Quotient (SQ) eventually.

Known struggles we go through integrating personal and professional lives:
- Blockage of creativity and innovative thinking.
- Ever-growing relationship conflicts.
- Fighting internal resistance to change.
- Lack of self-esteem.
- Limited physical and mental energy resources.
- Underdeveloped self-knowledge.
- Resistance moving towards psychological integration and wholeness.
- Being stuck with experiencing emotions like ego, fear, pride, arrogance, greed, anger, envy, lust, anger, etc. at unhealthy levels.

The capability we need to fight those struggles:

- Gaining knowledge of self through self-discovery & self-awareness.
- Practicing unwavering self-honesty.
- Cultivating self-compassion.
- Reclaiming projections again and again.
- Keeping a record of our discoveries.

Beliefs of aspects that spirituality cultivates deeply:
- Healthy self-esteem.
- Personal accountability & management.
- Thinking rationally, realistically, inwardly & outwardly, expansive perspectives.
- Appropriate discernment.

Values that spirituality cultivates deeply:
- Compassion
- Discipline
- Kindness
- Humility
- Love
- Integrity
- Resilience
- Determination
- Grit
- Perseverance
- Patience
- Honesty
- Endurance
- Tolerance
- Mutual respect, trust, and flexibility.
- Focus, attention, and adaptability.

Skills that spirituality cultivates deeply:
- Comfortable being uncomfortable.
- Problem solving.
- Planning.
- Organizing.
- A new outlook on boredom and motivation.
- Creativity.
- Curiosity to learn and grow in the positive direction.
- Short-term focus with long-term thinking.
- Finding opportunities and seeing them through desired outcomes.

How do I Practice Spirituality?

From my childhood experience growing up in a spiritual household in India, I recall that the entire home environment was cultivated to practice daily routines that supported spirituality. I was a blind follower then, as there was no knowledge or understanding provided to know why I was doing what I was doing. Like most of my generation, I just had to do as asked. Soon, during my early adulthood years, I fluctuated my beliefs from being an atheist to being an agnostic. Until a time came when I pacified all my curiosity about life and questioned them deeply, to become a believer eventually, and now a spiritual practitioner. What changed within me was the understanding that choosing spirituality is a path of choosing optimism versus choosing to take a pessimistic viewpoint of life. Pessimism is where the existence of everything, including life, is regarded as either

- Being a matter of random chance or
- Being engrossed in living the material reality only or
- Our existence justified through the use of dry matter-based philosophies or
- Concocting life philosophies based on randomized reasoning as we deem fit.

- Remaining intentionally or unintentionally stuck at a point to convince oneself not to pursue spirituality. By giving oneself reasons to have all the physical proofs of the existence of higher realities beforehand so that one can start moving the needle forward and take a chance for their life, in their life!

In my world, the clarity & knowledge I gained reading bona fide ancient texts of wisdom, experiences that my practices offered, self-reflection that helped me better understand myself, and access to the community I received so far from my spiritual journey have been enough proof to continue on this path of optimism. It has proved to be the missing link in many individuals' lives for centuries, and it has also done so for me. Because they chose optimism, they never stopped objectively questioning to find their right path. While on their path, they found answers to their assumptions and never let any doubt shatter their faith in the process. Spirituality need not be vague, lacking in action or efforts, requiring cumbersome rituals or practice within the bounds of extreme seclusion. But it can be integrated into our daily functioning of life. Integrating deeper meaning to life effortlessly, helping it be the essence of what you do, the purpose of what you do, and the heart & soul of what you do.

I am thankful for the blessing that I chose such a wonderful opportunity to live a human life in the right way.

Spirituality can give us great short-term and long-term progressive outcomes when practiced properly, some of which we discussed earlier in this chapter. Most importantly, spirituality infuses the right motivation to keep up with practicing genuine emotional intelligence (not cognitive empathy), cultivate strength of the heart, and perform one's duty compassionately, devoid of unhealthy attachments & desires. If professionals follow such practices in their daily lives, they can collectively resolve issues of struggling with managing unpleasant experiences & behaviors. This brings positive effects in their personal lives and benefits working dynamics and culture at the workplace, infusing values of humility, compassion, honesty, and integrity. Having said that, any spiritual practices done voluntarily will eventually help rather than seemingly doing it for the sake of it because you are asked to do so. You can practice objective curiosity to find clarity and incrementally experiment with practices to eventually cultivate voluntary integration of spirituality into your life. You may have any spiritual practices or paths that you are exploring or working for you; the goal is to develop love and deep acknowledgment of active functioning of a higher reality in the present moment by undertaking service in your endeavors. I spoke about one of the streams of yoga, i.e., bhakti-yoga, which worked for me as a path to explore and integrate spirituality into my daily life. The goal is not to debate which discipline of spirituality is the best but to keep exploring multiple paths, one at a time, before finding the one that works for you. The goal is to start with building just enough care, to even care about spirituality. Explore with the path available or known to you. One must exhibit at least some curiosity and exercise it through a bona fide spiritual mentor of that discipline. A spiritual mentor can provide you with the right information to answer your questions & assumptions and guide you through a path, knowledge, and practices at your level to reach a specific spiritual goal. Cultivating values, character, and behaviors aligned simply with your vision, mission, and objectives can be challenging to sustain but made easy by following practices of spiritual discipline.

Steadily, spiritual practices can become your life's new religion. Many get confused between religion & spirituality, and they are often misunderstood. They are terms used interchangeably to refer to one another. But in reality, they are interlinked in harmonious ways. Individuals who follow religion aren't always found to be spiritual, but it is always true that those who practice spirituality are religious. Spirituality is the practice of philosophy and the basis for every self-regulatory act. Religiosity is the act of following processes, methods, and daily practices. Adopting various methods to practice philosophy formulates a religion that is built to reveal spiritual knowledge & experience of true happiness. This makes the practitioner leap beyond, getting caught in the mechanical nature of the practices themselves and overtly focusing on the outcomes they offer. Without religiously following spiritual practices (based on your chosen spiritual paths), there is a grim possibility of growing your spiritual quotient; just knowing information & being knowledgeable is not enough. This is true for any endeavor we undertake in our day-to-day lives.

Spirituality changes our consciousness and not just the mindset. Spirituality makes one compassionate beyond just being emotionally intelligent. Spirituality makes mundane enjoyment & burdens of responsibility into joyful service & duty. Spirituality gives us a chance to elevate our thinking to gain knowledge of being human beyond seeking ordinary outcomes. Spiritual practices, when understood rightly and done incrementally over a period of time, can naturally cultivate intentions & focus on doing good, contributing with love & devotion, compassion, and kindness. Progressively building a spiritual quotient can become one's second nature. Integrating spirituality through our practices and preserving it for life can make our endeavors truly successful, meaningful, and blissful. Not forgetting, in the journey, we receive the valuable gifts of a well-developed positive character that we respect & practice and a vision for ourselves, which may be difficult yet joyfully attainable!

Practice time. Let's get to it!

1. Individuals
    a. Work through your answers related to self-discovery and self-knowledge questions posed in this chapter.
    b. Follow through practice to keep up with building your spiritual connection with yourself. Some of the things one can do are
        i. Find a spiritual mentor (from your chosen discipline) to identify & work through your spiritual goals.
        ii. Adopt a clean, organic, non-violent & simple lifestyle. Refer to more practices mentioned in *Chapter - Power of Health!*
        iii. Based on the spiritual orientation of your choice, include daily practices.
        Ones that are recommended here are from Bhakti Yoga discipline, which provides for daily practices like gratitude prayers, meditation, reading, hearing, and understanding life philosophy through spiritual scriptures, performing exercises to keep bodily well-being like yoga and breathing techniques, practicing mindfulness techniques, and working to meditate from 10 minutes with exponentially increasing time to 120 minutes (based on what can be permitted in your committed time).
        iv. Include spiritual tourism in your yearly travel plan.
        v. Indulge in spiritual retreats as and when required.

2. Teams, Organizations
    a. Keep workspaces inclusive to embrace professionals practicing spirituality (not keeping any distinction between followed disciplines and practices) in their daily lives.
    b. On the subject of Spirituality and/or Life Philosophy, empower employees to schedule training, invite guest speakers, schedule brainstorming sessions, and encourage forming in-house communities to exchange different

viewpoints, practices, and benefits to learn from and improve group or team-level collaboration.
c. Introduce employee benefits that offer to support engaging in spiritual retreats.

CHAPTER 12

Power of Health

'Health is a state of complete harmony of the body, mind, and spirit. When one is free from physical disabilities and mental distractions, the gates of the soul open.'

- B. K. S. Iyengar, Indian Teacher of Yoga and Author

After returning from my recent work trip to the United Kingdom and wrapping up a successful customer visit, I resumed office in India. The project work consumed me and the team, preparing for this new customer's upcoming software project delivery. Times were hectic and occupied with work, planning, learning, and due diligence. As the days passed by, I felt a subtle drag every day. My appetite had gone for a toss, and I could see a few physical changes cropping up. For the first time, my weight had bumped by 5 to 7 kgs, and my skin was going darker than it had been earlier. For the most part, like many individuals, I also thought this was probably some random weight gain due to eating out during my recent work trip abroad. So I need not feel concerned and get on with life as usual. But the feeling of being dragged only increased day after day. Supplementing vitamin deficiencies did not help, nor did any amount of fresh air, change in routine, exercise, or eating home-cooked food. Adding it up, a month later, I experienced extreme fatigue and could not move out of bed or even do any everyday tasks. And there I found my nails chipping away! Thanks to WebMD quizzes I loved taking for over a decade, I instantly knew that there was something deeply wrong than I had anticipated. My body was giving me some signals, which I was conveniently ignoring by giving legitimately sounding rational reasons.

This time, I paid attention and consulted the doctor. My world collapsed when I got to see my blood work. I had contracted a disease for the first time in thirty years. I thought I had less time and could not comprehend anything positive about the situation. This is how dying feels like, I wondered. I decided to take it in stride. As I could hardly do anything to reverse the damage it had caused. I was suffering from an endocrine disorder. I instinctively jumped to find out every piece of information that I could about endocrine diseases. And I did, despite being down the drain in my weakness. The disease was caused by prolonged unmanaged stress. For most endocrinologists (specialist doctors in endocrine system gland disorders), this is as normal as getting the flu in the body. Fighting some normal inflammation. I was happy to learn from an expert specialist that it wouldn't be as bad as I thought and that it would pass as time passed. All I had to do was pop a pill every morning on an empty stomach, and I could get on with my life as if nothing bad had ever happened to me. I was relieved!

Years passed, and with this practice, I struggled to keep my weight & energy in check. I kept myself knowledgeable about what was happening within my body. And how can I maintain good health? I adopted several healthy diets and routines, which helped, but every now and then, my lingering fatigue will come back. Maintaining my motivation was hard and often affected my engagements at work. Through times of struggle at work, I kept hearing those voices asking me, 'Woman, work it out!'. Thankfully, it didn't affect my self-esteem, as hormonal changes are notoriously famous for doing through Thyroid disorder. I continuously worried that the not-so-normal state of body energy was making me uncomfortable. In those days, I had fatigue most of the day, which only I could feel and realize. No one else could figure out if anything was really out of place with me as I contained it within. Erratic work schedules contributed to my irregular sleep patterns. Other symptoms popping up more evidently now, like tingling, cold, numbness in hands & feet, unhealthy cholesterol levels, drying skin, and frequent brain fog. I never thought a so-called normal disease, sitting quietly within me, was dictating my energy source as my adrenals were fatigued more often than any normal person would experience. Continuing to pop a pill every day, which didn't seem to do any good, I felt helpless.

Helpless but not losing hope, there came a time when I decided to take the route to adopt veganism for environmental reasons. Within 6 to 8 months, the anti-inflammatory whole foods plant-based diet and mild body exercise routine greatly helped me. It got my old, normal self back. All my vitals were functioning optimally, and lab reports showed results like that of an 8-year-old girl. I truly, for the first time, was performing at my best! My mental faculties were functioning at their highest as they were getting the cleanest source of supply through plant-based whole foods. Physically, I felt more energized and could manage to do more than I had ever done. My fatigue was non-existent, and I slept like a baby, on time, every day. Overall, I was surprised by the experience & effects of natural clean living on my health. This was a lesson in disguise to discover how optimal health played the most powerful role in my life, as I was busy taking care of personal and professional responsibilities and rushing through daily life. I decided to help others take advantage of learning from my experience. After getting myself certified in Plant-based nutrition by T. Colin Campbell through eCornell University (the body which conducted the largest ever nutrition research in the world called *The China Study*), I soon started this pioneering community based out of India focused on Whole Foods Plant-based Lifestyle, WholeWay! This was when veganism, a sub-stream of plant-based diets, was about to become a worldwide mass phenomenon. It was a deeply gratifying experience to channel my learning to make a change in others' lives. Many who joined the community benefited through online guided challenges and offline workshops. I wanted to spread the message that under the rut of furthering our desires, ambition, achievements, success, goals, dreams, visions, and happiness, we all somewhere truly neglect the most wonderful aspect of our lives.

The power of our Health!

Total Health worked for me, focusing on bodily, mental, and spiritual aspects. Adopting a lifestyle that gave it meaning and let it shape good health. It was no longer an impossible dream that I couldn't achieve. I understood how to treat this instrument of the human body to deliver the most priced purpose we want to live by. At the outset, like everyone, I also knew the benefits of keeping good health. But having experienced what I did and internalizing what I learned, I now had all the ingredients and recipes to be healthy; I was practicing them daily and happily!

I reflected on this journey and kept myself authentic and in check about the lessons I learned during this time. Health is basic and essential to us, yet most of us living in urban cities choose to treat our bodies like garbage bins (I couldn't find another suitable analogy to describe how our bodies might feel). Be it by daily, systematic dumping of high amounts of caffeine, unhealthy fats, and refined, deep-fried, sugar-laden foodstuffs. Or succumbing to the temptations to try out every new trendy restaurant or cuisine around the block. Or by exposure to various types of toxins that are coming from intoxicants like alcohol, active or passive smoking, environment, EMFs, modern-day products that we use, etc. Or putting in stress-inducing excessive hours at work without adequate rest. Or doing an unnecessary amount of body workout. In the name of world modernization, such widely adopted lifestyles are progressively changing our immediate lives towards poor health.

At the workplace, most of what we promote as a culture of convenience is nothing but hurting our health and testing our capabilities to control our minds from temptations. The disadvantage of giving autonomy of choice amongst numerous temptations is that choices can be easily exploited to our detriment. Capacity to take control over our urges that none of us have enough left after being glued to the back-to-back working sessions on our respective computers and constant exposure to over-the-top amounts of EMFs using our handheld devices. Whose responsibility is it to take care of our health optimally? Primarily, it's ours, but our surroundings can immensely help if they are kept in check & conducive enough to promote good health. Having said that, this is nowhere suggesting creating an autocratic, unjust, and forceful environment but focusing on infusing creative solutions to present healthier choices. As we spend most of our day at the workplace, one legitimate question to ask is how much of our corporate life positively supports us in focusing on our health. Yes, most of us carry many essential health benefit plans through our respective organizations, but is that enough?

- What about those vending machines staring at us to splurge on packaged foods when we are casually passing by?
- What about the exposure to air conditioning that we dry out our bodies from?
- What about those unhealthy fats & sugar-laden foods served at the counter?
- What about the active or passive smoking breaks that one is exposed to?
- What about the intake of coffee cups in the name of breakout talks?
- What about alcohol and the amount of food intake we are exposed to when we celebrate our wins together?
- What about our dietary choices affecting our nervous system systematically, agitating our minds, and having a deeper impact on our emotional regulation, e.g., showing microaggressions?

Keeping the workplaces fun, quirky, and filled with tempting goodies (or not-so-goodies) only lures professionals for some time. As in life, everything is temporary, so do these seemingly fun and interesting conveniences. As professionals, our most energetically active hours of the day are spent at the workplace. If organizations and individuals can adopt and welcome this change, knowing it's a long-term, game-changing proposition, we can all practice, work & live at our best. It has the power to uplift our motivations, rigor, alertness, focus, concentration, attention, engagement, fulfillment, activeness, and productivity. Most importantly, conserving our energy resources throughout the day to easily accommodate space for our personal lives equally into our day's plan. No one would want to exhaust, burn out, and feel down the drain by the end of the day to meet, greet, and spend time with their near and dear ones with the least vigor in them.

Simply, the combination of physical, mental, and spiritual health ensures one can benefit from maintaining good, balanced health. The crucial missing piece comes from our personal endeavors, but it is critical that modern-day work cultures create supportive environments. The focus on health starts at the will of an individual but should not just stay there. Organizations can very well take steps to assist their workforce in staying in the right direction by giving more choices that are healthier. They can expand the boundaries of benefits offered through health policies like health checkups, lab tests, and hospitalization expense claims, which are essential but BAU constructs. While they are important, the focus is on occasional usage. These will not draw results for organizations to truly help & assist their workforce in increasing their tenure affinity, their daily productive engagements with teams, and their contributions to organizations at large. Policies focusing on micro-engagements related to healthy well-being practices in daily life can progressively help professionals improve their performance & positive engagement within the company, teams, or groups. Resulting in professionals feeling genuinely cared for by the organization and vested in their lives beyond just a transactional service & compensation.

Health is key! Having good health offers more benefits in the professional arena than we all can cumulatively understand. None of us need to wait & experience an extremely negative episode of deteriorating health in our life to finally make us understand and take a step towards a mindful practice of a good lifestyle. We don't need to wait to make a change until something irreversible hits us badly, making us live a compromising life course. Lifestyle is such an ingrained integral part of our being that it directly drives our wellness and longevity, which, in effect, will make us successful in our personal and professional endeavors. All one needs to do is start by changing one's outlook on health and what it brings to the table in our daily lives and the long run. There are many options out there providing solutions for total health. From ancient wisdom to modern science to hybrid approaches, one can learn, explore, experiment, sustain, see results, and practice what suits each of us. Guidance captured through the practice time exercise in this chapter suggests one such starter approach. Knowing that the change at the body, mind, and soul levels collectively can do wonders for our overall health and well-being, it can provide us with the vitality and vigor needed to pursue our dreams.

Practice time. Let's get to it!

1. Individuals

   Consider three main aspects of total health and list the bare minimum practices to follow from each sub-category. In case you have a prediagnosed health condition, then it is advisable to practice appropriate discernment and/or consult a relevant physician before practicing any guidance shared here.

   Body
   1. Rise
      a. Early, before 6 AM every day.
   2. Move
      a. Move your body twice a day, once in the morning daylight and once at night time.
      b. At least for 20 minutes a day.
      c. Moving could include walking, running, swimming, dancing, yoga, stretching, or sports. Choose what works best for your body constitution.
   3. Eat
      a. Regularly practice eating whole foods & plant-based meals more often.
      b. Foods to include healthy fats, protein, carbs, nuts & seeds, and supplements. Skip nothing, as they all have their role to play. Avoid foods agitating the nervous system, like Allium family vegetables, and drinks containing neurotoxins like caffeine, alcohol, etc.
      c. To increase your affinity towards specific diet choices, learn more about the foods you eat and the lifestyle you practice.
      d. Effectively practice moderation and mindfulness while eating. Regulate the number of meals a day, time, portion of the meals, and occasional fasting.
   4. Rest
      a. Throughout the day, when you feel tired or weary, rest for

15 to 20 minutes.
- b. Sleep early, before 10 PM every night.
- c. Take mindful rest breaks.
- d. Avoid rushing through the day to manage increased nervous energy within the body.
- e. Practice 1 hour of downtime before sleeping hours.

Mind

1. Learn
   - a. Learn something every day, spending 15 minutes.
   - b. Practice your microlearning.
   - c. Cultivate the habit of reading regularly.
   - d. Document and/or share your learning.
2. Focus, Attention
   - a. Create a tranquil space in your brain by practicing meditation techniques.
   - b. Starting with 5 to 20 minutes per day in the morning.
3. Engage
   - a. Recreational activities like nature travel, spiritual retreats, hobbies like soothing creative arts, music, etc.
   - b. Spend time with your loved ones and those near you. Among family, friends, and other relationships.
   - c. Keep a journal logging highlights and thoughts for the day.
   - d. Focus your energies inwards more than outwards, i.e., overthinking what others think of you is a lost cause.
   - e. Be mindful of the content you consume through television shows, movies, videos, photos, books, etc. Your choices in this matter can significantly affect the health of your nervous system, either soothing or agitating it.

Soul
1. Practice active spirituality, i.e., cultivate a spiritual practice routine containing reading, meditating, and giving through serving.
2. Practice morning & evening prayers of gratitude.
3. Practice morning & evening breathing exercises and meditation practices.
4. Read ancient texts of wisdom.
5. Regularly serving in local communities or spiritual groups. And visits to high-positive energy places.
6. Understand the difference between being thankful and grateful. Practice both every day.

2. Teams
   a. Promote clean eating celebrations by adopting plant-based food feasts without neurotoxins like caffeine, alcohol, smoking, etc.
   b. Replace smoking with alternatives to control the urge, like practicing meditation & yoga techniques to contain the urge for a more extended period.
   c. Celebrate health days twice or thrice a week.

3. Organizations
   a. Promote neurotoxins-free pantry counters or vending machines, i.e., caffeine-free and alcohol-free. Start by adopting herbal drinks as an alternative.
   b. Offering total health training & workshops for employees that focus on integrative approaches to manage wellness at body, mind, and soul levels.
   c. Organize workshops for mindfulness techniques and meditation practices to reduce & manage stress, anxiety, and burnout.
   d. Celebrate health days twice or thrice a week.
   e. Rethink benefits to include mental & emotional well-being workshop vouchers or as a reimbursable expense.

PART V

The Bridge

'I've concluded that the metric by which God will assess my life isn't dollars but the individual people whose lives I've touched.'

- Clayton Christensen, American Academic and Business Consultant

How can one get their head around everything that you have practiced so far through this book? Bringing it all in can be a challenge. The practice time exercises most definitely led you into thinking and discovery mode. Also, compelling you to spend time to prioritize the list you have worked on so far. It can be overwhelming to look at the list and have some self-doubts.

- Will I be able to achieve it all?
- Is it worth my time and energy?
- Why focus on this when I have plenty of things to do anyway?

The only answer to these doubts is that you are worth living a life made up of your dreams and experiencing meaningful success. In that process, you become a fine individual and improve the surrounding environment, community, and world. Isn't that an appealing thought in itself? If not, then consider this one. We go through ups and downs in our daily lives, having to experience wins and losses of magnitude, small or large. If we only focus on the wins, life can get too boring and predictable because we, as humans, strive to create meaningful experiences based on our endeavors. And if we have only challenges, we may struggle to come out being hopeful & happy. The path from living reality to living dreams while being your dream is the path that guarantees a middle way to reach your goals optimally.

By putting in hours to read through this book so far and working through all the practice time exercises, the list of your goals and dreams is right there within the reach of your hands. Now, all you need is to know how to approach it systematically and work its way through. Leaping the initial hiccup of self-doubt and motivation gap, you can keep these goals at arm's reach or on your desk or an accessible cue card that can help you repeatedly see them and remind yourself of your destination. This is a good start for staying motivated and crossing the chasm to take the required action and stay on course. It would be good to revisit your work on developing Intrinsic & Extrinsic motivation from *Chapter - Motivation* to address any motivation gap.

You may find yourself not knowing, at times, what steps to take and move forward, or wanting to learn a few things to contribute well to the goal, or seeking to build a team of trusted & passionate enthusiasts who wish to work on similar goals, or finding yourself in the middle of opportunities that make you fearful. Thinking, 'What if I do not sail through this? It's completely new, and I haven't done it before.'. These are opportunities to unlearn, relearn, think, contemplate, plan, organize, act, experience, and grow through your endeavor. While it'll require your commitment, resilience, and focus, it'll provide you with the gifts of values and experiences you can latch on for the rest of your life. Whatever may be your purpose, known / unknown / yet to be discovered, you will get one step closer to it. Making this endeavor worth living for and setting an exemplary example for others to follow by living it. Pursuing it is the best proposition over staying where you are.

Without a set of priorities and what matters the most, say a master plan, principles, and a framework, all that you have discovered so far through your introspection & working along the guidance of practice time exercises can remain just a set of paper-written goals. It can be transformed into the tangible outcomes you aspire for, keeping you motivated throughout your professional journey. I have undergone transformations in phases while working with enterprises of different scales. During the initial phase of five years of empowerment, I was dabbling with whatever work & experiences came my way, not knowing what opportunity or experience would take me to which destination. In the second phase of the next ten years of transformation, my hardships and experiences got tougher but were worth every second of the challenge thrown my way, many of which you have already read through this book, and they led me to build the foundation required to achieve my long-standing dreams. The rear end of five years was the beginning of evolution, finding the real treasure and turning every opportunity into success.

My professional journey would have been different if I had adequate support from peers & leaders, found myself help in the form of mentors or coaches early, and had the maturity to take the right lessons from adverse or good times. However, not having this support allowed me to figure out things independently as I went along. It forced me to develop a framework that worked for me and many others I worked with. Now, you can take advantage of it at any stage that you are in. Right here, right now! The framework can lead any professional's life into a harmonious working environment, keeping an eye on the prize and having everything they set out to achieve. You need not wait and figure it out on your own, but start from where this book guidance can lead you.

It'll be an adventure worth taking! And it starts at an individual level, with you.

PART VI

The Plan!

'Good fortune is what happens when opportunity meets with planning.'

- Thomas Edison, American Inventor and Businessman

Most live the reality, many live their dreams, and a handful be the dreams they aspire to. What makes only a few and not everyone think about, know of, and work towards achieving their dreams? Why is it random that some individuals are seemingly successful at achieving their goals and appear happier than others? What do they know or do differently than others to have it all?

Availability or accessibility to differentiating factors like mindset, social environment, education, resources, role models, life circumstances, etc., frequently contributes to one's progress. Do these individuals also know in advance

- (WHAT) What matters the most to achieve and call a successful life?
- (WHY) Why to prioritize what they do?
- (HOW) How do you work through it?

These questions represent the WHAT, WHY, and HOW of achieving a prosperous, meaningful & happy life.

While you have worked through WHAT you should focus on by following practice time exercises, let's focus on the model & framework to put all of that into a strategy that talks about WHY and HOW parts.

CHAPTER 13

The Master Model

'Everything should be made as simple as possible, but not simpler.'

- Albert Einstein, German-born American Theoretical Physicist

For most of us, we struggle with identifying our WHY, the reason to pursue anything in life. For small matters, we may know the whys, e.g., why do we choose to eat certain foods frequently? It could be because it gives us a sense of satisfaction and pleasure or improves our health so that we can keep up with our journey. But when it comes to our entire life course, one must be intentional about identifying the purpose of living it. Going deeper and knowing why we dream of something that we do can make our endeavor to pursue goals very clear to us. With this clarity, we make the process of achieving those dreams more engaging, wholehearted, and worthwhile. For anyone to do this effectively, it is essential to have access to a well-researched model. A model that can guide us through aspects that are positive & essential for humankind. A model that can make identifying (WHY) our purpose with a more approachable process meant for the masses. A well-defined model, which has worked time & again, that clearly aligns with one's goals and is easy to follow so that everyone can benefit from it.

One such model is what we discussed in the earlier *Chapter - Uncovering the Truth!* It is called *Maslow's Hierarchy of Needs* by Dr. A. H. Maslow; this can be a good starting point. It can guide us to follow a generalized model to identify our needs and what we value the most as a human species. It can also help us identify and categorize our life goals from basic to advanced stages of human needs. For example, from the most primary basic needs to psychological needs to the highest need of self-fulfillment, i.e., achieving fulfillment by reaching our full potential. This fundamental life strategy must be curated before altering it to accommodate our professional goals.

The following table shows the *Work IT Out - Master Model for Categorizing Human Needs and Goals and Aligning them to Purpose*. It covers high-level categories and respective detailed needs that Maslow's hierarchy suggests to work towards. To further simplify *Maslow's Hierarchy of Needs*, it can be correlated with the *PERMA-V Model of Positive Psychology in Practice*, which stands for Positivity, Engagement, Relationships, Meaning, Achievement, and Vitality. Together, they clarify what factors in life one can pursue, what priority one may follow, and how individual goals align with these respective needs.

For example, you identified some goals working through practice time exercises from *Chapter - Motivation*; those goals can be categorized as one's psychological needs of esteem affecting positive emotions, vitality, and facilitating achievement in one's life.

Another example is if you identified goals to streamline your physical health routine from *Chapter - Power of Health!* Then those goals can be categorized as fulfilling one's most basic need of physiological wellness, addressing warmth & rest, and affecting vitality in one's life.

All the categories and respective detailed factors with needs mentioned in the following *Work IT Out - Master Model* are well-researched to have a greater positive impact and effect on our quality of life. Not just through individual experiences of many, talking of a few of them, it is researched that significant partners, children, friends, sports, spirituality, community involvement, salaries, savings, nutrition, optimal rest & leisure, etc., contribute to life satisfaction. Not surprisingly, health problems harm our quality of life. Other studies have found that practicing kindness, mindfulness, meditation, care, and gratefulness can improve life to a higher degree. Cultivating lighthearted humor and laughter, dedicating time to learning, and developing a growth mindset (believing that your abilities and life can improve through effort and persistence, refer to *Chapter - Mindset*) can help support our essential esteem needs. Such research-backed observations can give us more than enough assurance and room to develop a starter blueprint based on these models. A blueprint that works for everyone, categorizing their needs and mapping them to their goals.

Category of Needs		Work IT Out - Master Model Guiding Principles	Maslow's Hierarchy of Needs	PERMA-V Factors
Self-fulfillment Needs	Self-Actualization	Vision Health Way of Working	Desire to become the most one can be. • Achieving one's full potential / Morality, Acceptance, Experience purpose, Meaning and inner potential, Spontaneity • Creativity • Life-enhancer: Kindness, Gratefulness, Compassion, Care, Mindfulness & Meditation	• Meaning (contributing towards a better progressive world) • Vitality (being energetic and healthy) • Engagement (being in the flow and absorbed without accounting for time spent)
Psychological Needs	Self-Esteem	Competence Mindset	• Feelings of accomplishment / Confidence, The need to be a unique individual, Strength, Freedom, Self-esteem, Growth Mindset • Prestige / Achievement, Respect of others, Status, Recognition	• Positive emotions (frequent feelings of contentment and pleasure) • Achievement (attaining goals, striving for success) • Vitality (being energetic and healthy) • Sports, laughter & humor, leisure & creative activities
	Love & Belonging	Culture Relationships	• Intimate Relationships / Family, Significant Partners • Friendship • Sense of connection / Intimacy, Community involvement	• Positive emotions (frequent feelings of contentment and pleasure) • Relationships (mutual feelings of support, love, and care) • Vitality (being energetic and healthy)
Basic Needs	Safety & Security	Health Relationships	• Safety / Health, Family - children/ parents/ siblings & social abilities • Security / Personal Security, Resources, Employment, Property, Salaries, Savings	• Achievement (attaining goals, striving for success) • Vitality (being energetic and healthy)
	Physiological Needs	Health	• Warmth / Air, Food, Water, Shelter, Clothing, Nutrition • Rest / Sleep, Mindfulness, Meditation • Reproduction	• Vitality (being energetic and healthy)

Work IT Out - Master Model for Categorizing Human Needs and Goals and Aligning them to Purpose. Inspired by Maslow's Hierarchy of Needs and PERMA-V Model.

Planning for your path to success in the personal & professional arena requires knowing the aspects to prioritize and knowing them beforehand rather than figuring everything out as life progresses through our individual experiences. Here are the seven most essential *Work IT Out - Master Model Guiding Principles* that highlight which aspects are important to focus on so that one can *Live & Be the Dream while Living Reality*.

I. Health

Health is a primal thing that we all depend on. Our fundamental need in life that lets us function personally and professionally. From the ancient to the modern era, the definition of health has changed progressively. For better or for worse, it is a subjective opinion. However, we see the effects of having good health on our overall functioning in daily life and in the long run. Having good health can entail having vitality, vigor, and maintaining longevity. The same can be achieved through maintaining a good balance between three main factors of our health, i.e.,

- Physical health
- Mental health, broadly sub-divided into
    - Mental health
    - Emotional health
    - Psycho-physical health
- Spiritual health

Today, most of us focus predominantly on maintaining physical health. We are gearing up to acknowledge the need to have facilities & services readily available in other factors to maintain overall good health, which one can refer to as Total Health.

Our needs of food, water, air, shelter, clothing, and adequate rest can relate to having good physical health. Good mental health can translate into having healthy acceptance, love, connection, and capabilities within us, which can help us experience positive emotions and a steady state of mind. Mental health premise can hold us accountable for keeping ourselves well-confident, believing in ourselves, showing love & compassion towards ourselves and others, exercising the proper discernment and resilience based on the situation, etc. These can be an outcome of a healthy mental state. Mental health is also a function of our experiences imprinted in us while growing up that form the beliefs and values we exercise while making decisions, how we live our lives, and the approach to living life, etc. Such outlooks can be cultivated into optimistic, realistic, and rational mindsets with the help of various psychotherapy modalities if required. Working through our needs, thoughts, emotions, feelings & beliefs and keeping them reasonable & realistic can be a skill that can optimize our mental health wellness. In addition to accessing psychotherapy from practicing psychologists, lifestyle coaching is another way to identify such needs and work with specialized coaches or trained professionals to keep our mental health and well-being in check. With our physical health in reasonably good shape, we stay adequately focused and attentive to professional work. Professional work can help us meet our material needs by earning monetary outcomes, getting by in the daily course of life, planning for the future through savings, building skills, gaining time freedom, having a sense of achievement, etc. Which becomes furthermore approachable with a positive mindset, bringing stability to our lives. So, the ones who practice self-courage and seek help to support mental health wellness can likely have an advantage in approaching their life fully.

> *'Science makes things better, but spirituality should make people better through character transformation.'*
>
> *- S. B. Keshava Swami, Spiritual Author, Community Mentor, Dynamic Teacher*

Availability of proper physical health can also ensure our progress toward spiritual pursuits. Practicing religiosity has made it possible to sustain spiritual infusion in our lives for a long time. In today's time, with an excessive focus on material progression in life, the daily practice of spiritual disciplines is somehow waning out, which is the essence of cultivating religious practices. Through these, one can stay connected to one's deeper self and higher purpose, and at the same time, one can optimally translate it into action through well-balanced physical health. Spiritual practices are the backbone of formulating your purpose & meaning, building your values, and cultivating character strength. All of this is helpful for humanity at large to advance in a positive direction, starting from an individual's progress. The positive effects of this are directly seen in our daily professional lives.

Spiritual well-being is increasingly becoming important for humans to cultivate love, compassion, humility, integrity, resilience, honesty, and further divine qualities. When spiritual practices are pursued for decades and practiced daily, they can result in gaining valuable assets of solid values and bring more profound satisfaction in living one's life purpose. The earlier we commence our journey, the better. These are the only aspects that stay with us through our life experiences; while the world changes around you, you are growing, grounded in higher realities. And so this deserves priority amongst all life's aspects.

II. Vision

Imagine a world where everyone around you, including yourself, is on a journey without a destination. It'll be so exciting, exhilarating, full of anticipation of the unknown and, at the same time, the fear of the unknown. What an adventure it would be! While it can be one way of living life, we humans are hardwired to experience stability by knowing what destination we are going towards, what goal we would like to work towards, what vision we would like to pursue, and what is our current mission in that endeavor. It gives us more positive anticipation, excitement, and an optimal sense of fear to want to embark on such a journey. Now, imagine what it is like to live through such a journey and live your dreams. Happy, blissful, satisfying, isn't it? Perhaps no! The proof of the pudding is in doing things rather than just imagining; it's in living through the process rather than just caring to reach a destination. Yes, no matter how much we like the anticipation of successfully reaching our destinations, what we like and truly absorb is the process rather than the momentary happiness that comes with achieving our visions or dreams. So, while it's equally important to develop your vision (which can be interchangeably used as dreams), align it to a mission & purpose. It is more important to enjoy the journey, keeping up with our anxieties of deep-seated fears and insecurities.

Defining your vision with a target of 5 to 10 Years horizon can be a good starting point. Mapping them with short-term missions, activities, teams, support, resources, and planning will turn them into actionable tasks that one can track regularly to keep moving forward. Getting the job done while keeping an eye on your goals is achieved by having some prior knowledge of where you are doing, what it will entail to get there, and how to get there. You won't need to figure out everything, but some details are essential to get started on this journey. Unless you have figured out your vision (a dream), purpose, mission, and goals, no amount of micro-strategies (that we spoke about through this book) can help you reach a more coherent and satisfying outcome.

III. Competence

The knowledge economy in which we function, there is no shortage of resources to gain information through books, web-based online content, classroom teachings, etc. In such a fast-paced and changing world of technology, everything seems to be changing every other second, which requires new skills to be developed. The challenge is not the accessibility of information anymore (thanks to Google's vision of democratizing information and the advent of the World Wide Web). We all can get hold of information that we need in a fraction of a second. But simply gaining information is further than learning a new skill. What we increasingly lack is knowing what is required to stay relevant, knowing which information is relevant for your advancement, finding or creating opportunities for developing skills from acquired information, the ability to find time & commitment to follow through, and an ability to manage our time free of distraction.

Building competence is a function of knowing what is important to support your mission & vision and the task at hand. And which skills are relevant for them to be cultivated. Applying creativity, innovative thinking, an incremental growth mindset, and exploring more interesting opportunities to invite others to contribute are a part of the progression. Focusing on those things that matter the most over a period of time can build one's competence. Competence is the culmination of all these aspects; it's a process of continual learning and building skills to stay relevant while having fun at it.

IV.   Mindset

We discussed cultivating a growth mindset and its importance in *Chapter - Mindset*. Beyond that, one outlook that can work and help everyone in their journey is to become optimally self-sufficient steadily. Optimal Self-sufficiency is about being reliant on yourself, which can help you cut through tough times when adequate support or resources are unavailable. It makes you jump into the arena without having to struggle to deal with fears and insecurities of not being good enough, which greatly consumes the physical, mental, and spiritual energies of anyone. Remember that extreme self-sufficiency, or avoiding any form of help or support from our environment, is not what is suggested or referred to here. This skill of being optimally self-sufficient can be thought of as being an Intrapreneur in your own life. Intrapreneurs do not necessarily do everything by themselves; they still require connections, support, and resources from their surroundings. However, they excel in making headway for themselves by identifying the right opportunities to align with their life missions. They take along like-minded individuals eyeing for similar goals and make everyone's lives purposeful. They walk the talk, act respectfully, execute collaboratively, think objectively, execute with resilience, and deliver qualitatively. That's the hack! Being an Intrapreneur in your life and if everyone practiced this mindset, the world would truly see the meaning of individual & collective progress, collaboration, teamwork, deep connection & belonging.

V. Culture

Culture is widely defined as an amalgamation of elements like values, boundaries, and activities. *Values* contain language, ideas, and beliefs; *Boundaries* contain customs, codes, and institutions; *Activities* contain tools, techniques, works of art, rituals, and ceremonies, among other elements.

How does this definition translate to our life's purpose? The symbiotic relationship between what we call the culture of being is shaped through cultivating *Values* for building a fine character. We discussed essential and useful values across professional life experiences in *Chapter - Values for Character*. Identifying and building values that aid in functioning well within your boundaries is crucial. Your *Boundary* is the mission in the short term and vision in the long term, which is helping you focus & act appropriately to serve your current & future goals. Based on your identity, the values you would like to cultivate may vary, but considering values that match the requirements of the task at hand could also help you develop a fine character progressively. Additionally, a culture could benefit from *Activities* that are naturally creative and pleasurable. This can help bring dimensions of openness, acceptance, diversity & inclusion and to build camaraderie.

Culture needs us, and we need culture. Without culture, no finite definition of growth is achieved in any endeavor. Culture gives heart and soul to our journey through the values we exercise, the boundaries we function in, and the activities we undertake.

VI. Relationships

Numerous research through the decades have studied humans' lives and found a deep connection between having meaningful relationships with happiness & longevity of life. Relationships we experience through significant partners, familial - children/parents/siblings, friendships, and social community connections. All of which may or may not be on your list based on the meaning you'd derive from it, i.e., meaning derived from working through productive two-way exchanges, well-intentioned & well-meaning exchanges, social connectedness, and connection with thyself. Considering every individual has a unique identity, building and maintaining relationships can be challenging but, at the same time, rewarding. The more the spiritual quotient one develops, the easier it is to make meaningful relationships. This starts with developing the relationship one has with one's self. Having a learning attitude from adversities, one can set out to find and sustain meaningful relationships through life to feel a sense of connection, love, and belonging.

What we truly need is to change our mindset about looking at relationships, i.e., changing definitions of why relationships matter. For most of us, the riding thought to cultivate relationships is about, 'What can I eventually get from keeping this relationship?'. Instead, the perspective we need to develop is, 'I want to keep this relationship so that someone can have an avenue to explore if & when they need help.'. Developing harmonious relationships is lifelong work, and one should approach them with a service mindset, a mindset of duty, and a compassionate state of being for the highest fulfillment.

VII. Way of Working

Humans are creatures of habits, but until we develop habits that are good for us, we encounter a severe challenge of going through the change and sustaining it. Iteratively sustaining growth and making change is challenging, cumbersome, and sometimes tricky. Years of practiced perseverance, patience, commitment, and reliance on working methods can stall in a second if one encounters a lack of control over oneself. One can practice the process below to keep up with the change and sustenance cycle (refer to the illustration, *Way of Working - Wheel*). This method can also help us stay on course through such difficulties and pace ourselves toward progress.

A prerequisite for the process to work is to put yourself out there. One can do that by publicly sharing or anchoring the change they seek and figuring out an adequate team, resources, and support as they go along. One can adopt this cyclic process of approaching any task at hand, starting with reflection.

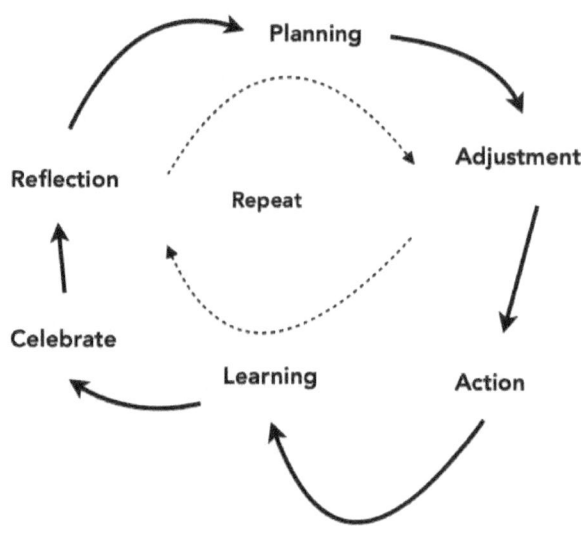

Way of Working - Wheel, inspired by Agile Methodology Sprint

The stages of this process include (mentioned in order):
1. **Reflection** - being mindful & clear of the task at hand.
2. **Planning** - planning for successful execution.
3. **Adjustment** - making adjustments to execution based on

prior knowledge or new learnings.
4. **Action** - taking action and sustaining it until done.
5. **Learning** - learning from outcome produced through action.
6. **Celebrate** - accepting the consequences through contemplation or rewarding efforts to continue.
7. **Repeat** - To adopt new learnings and make necessary amendments to the plan, repeating the stages starting from the reflection stage.

This way of working (method) can be applied to any set of tasks, problems, challenges, struggles, obstacles, mission, or vision to make incremental and informed progress. This can also help anyone stay objective, realistic, and rational during stressful circumstances.

While parallels between Maslow's hierarchy and PERMA-V model provide us with a *Work IT Out - Master Model* to categorize our needs and align our goals to them, *Work IT Out - Master Model Guiding Principles* help us keep focused on what is essential to prioritize. All of the priorities discussed in this chapter are the aspects that stay with you regardless of which organization, industry, geographical region, or changing era you function in. That is the foundation you build for your life, interleaving your personal and professional contexts together.

For now, let's absorb what we discussed in this chapter and take a breather from practice time.

CHAPTER 14

Work IT Out - Framework

'You don't have to be a genius or a visionary or even a college graduate to become successful. You just need a framework and a dream.'

- Michael Dell, American Billionaire Businessman and Investor

Now that you have worked through WHAT are your goals and WHY you wish to pursue them by using *Work IT Out - Master Model Guiding Principles*, let's understand HOW both learnings come together to create your individualized Work-life Strategy. After charting out a blueprint of needs and goals, the next step is to merge them into a working framework. The framework that aligns micro-strategies you've identified by working through each chapter's practice time exercises to your master model blueprint.

The following table shows the *Work IT Out - Framework* that can lead you to categorize your needs based on priorities and guided models discussed in the previous chapter. This framework can align your customized micro-strategies to your individualized purpose and vision. Micro-strategies are nothing but goals you identified from different chapter practice exercises through various stages of *Living the Reality*, *Living the*

Dream, and *Being the Dream*. For example, if you identified micro-strategies to streamline your mental health from *Chapters - Power of Health!* & *Uncovering the Truth!* Then, those micro-strategies can be categorized as addressing one's most basic need for physiological wellness to bring vitality to one's life. Focusing on the building blocks of body, mind, soul, and personal care.

One thing you need to curate rightly is your vision (dreams) and purpose. So that they can converge well into the *Work IT Out - Master Model & Framework* and give you maximum clarity to pursue goals on your way. You may ask how I can know if my dreams and purpose are appropriate. Largely, there are no dreams & purpose, right or wrong, where nothing is absolutely good or bad. Considering this, the only factor with which one can start to assess their purpose & dreams is how positively aligned they are to the overall impact they create in the world. Purpose and dreams can be different for everyone, and waiting to get them perfectly defined is not necessary. What works for you now may not work for you sometime in the distant future; that's the process of evolution. Then, would you rather confront it now or let it run your course? A better approach is to be intentional about defining your dreams and purpose, in whichever smaller capacity & clarity, and have them shape over time.

Also, some factors affect why we have different purposes and dreams than others. Generational changes and our surrounding environment play a huge role in knowing what matters to us. From Baby Boomers, Generation X, Millennials, and Generation Z to Generation Alpha, all of them influence & exhibit their share of strengths, successes, and challenges differently, which works to their advantage or disadvantage. This also affects their purpose and dreams to build a legacy for the next generation. Having said that, there is a common wisdom that cuts through generational gaps and offers us a way to streamline our purpose and dreams.

Work IT Out - Framework Process combines one's purpose, dreams (vision), needs, mission, goals, and micro-strategies.

Work IT Out - Framework

Purpose - Needs - Goals (WHY)	Work IT Out - Master Model Guiding Principles (WHAT)	By Focusing on Micro-strategies (HOW)	
		Work IT Out - Framework Building Blocks	Work IT Out - Framework Chapter Guidance (facilitating the WHY - Purpose, Needs, and Goals)
Goal: Being the Dream! Catering to the Self-fulfillment Needs • Self-Actualization • Meaning • Vitality • Engagement	Vision Health Way of Working	Learning Interests Spirituality Personal Care Community & Society	Guiding Chapters: • Uncovering the Truth! • Not just Intellect • Power of Health
Goal: Living the Dream! Catering to the Psychological Needs • Self-Esteem • Love & Belonging • Relationships • Vitality • Positive emotions • Achievement • Leisure & creative activities	Competence Mindset	Job Learning Finances Interests Entertainment Personal Care	Guiding Chapters: • Having it All! • The Skills Game • Values for Character • Work-Life Balance • Culture of Diversity
	Culture Relationships	Relationships Community & Society	Guiding Chapters: • Not just Intellect • Work-Life Balance • Culture of Diversity • Collaboration, Teamwork & Allyship
Goal: Living the Reality Catering to the Basic Needs • Safety & Security • Physiological Needs • Achievement • Vitality	Health Relationships	Relationships Job Finances Personal Care	Guiding Chapters: • Motivation • Mindset • Accountability • Collaboration, Teamwork & Allyship
	Health	Body Mind Spirituality Personal Care	Guiding Chapters: • Uncovering the Truth! • Power of Health

Work IT Out - Framework, inspired and revised based on Maslow's Hierarchy of Needs, PERMA-V Model. Key aspects are highlighted in bold letters.

Purpose - Needs - Goals (WHY): *Covers the purpose and goals catering to specific needs, making it clear WHY you are pursuing your endeavor.*

***Work IT Out - Master Model* Guiding Principles (WHAT):** *Covers which guiding principles to follow to achieve respective goals, making it clear WHAT you prioritize to pursue your endeavor.*

By Focusing on *micro-strategies (HOW): Covers correlated micro-strategies, which you have built working along practice time exercises against each chapter, making the list of activities to know HOW to pursue your respective goals, to fulfill relevant needs, and to realize your purpose.*

Work IT Out - Framework building blocks: *These building blocks provide a simplified terminology to understand high-level activity areas that are pursued to achieve goals.*

Work IT Out - Framework chapter guidance (facilitating the WHY - Purpose, Needs, and Goals): *This set of chapters provides a relevant list to curate respective micro-strategies required to pursue goals.*

How do we bring it all together?

*For example, if your **purpose** is to create harmonious relationships to create a sense of community in the world, then it would require you to pursue the stage (goal) of Living the Reality. To achieve this **goal**, you prioritize **guiding principles** of health and/or relationships. Focusing on the **building blocks** like relationships, jobs, personal care, and health at the body, mind, and spiritual levels. Micro-strategies you've identified from different **Chapters** (here Power of Health!, Uncovering the Truth!, Mindset, Motivation, Accountability, and Collaboration, Teamwork & Allyship are applicable) will allow you to curate a list of activities to pursue your goal and fulfill the purpose. Through this pursuit, you can cater to your basic **needs** of achievement, vitality, and physiological Needs.*

Work IT Out - Framework Process

Use *Worksheet: Work IT Out - Framework* to work through this section. To download it, refer to the *Resources* section of *Chapter - Your Journey*.

I. **Outline your Life Purpose.**

   Purpose serves as an important boundary for your strategy. It is a guiding north star for your personal & professional life. You have already followed *Work IT Out - Master Model Guiding Principles* from the previous chapter to define the initial drivers of things you value. You can further refine it by following the steps mentioned below to outline your Purpose. Your purpose and domain of influence lie at the intersection of answers to the questions below. Reflect on the answers to these questions, formulate an initial draft of your purpose, and seek feedback from others to develop your life purpose further.

   - **What are my strengths?** Most of us know of our strengths and seek help from colleagues at work, family, or friends to identify these in case additional help is required. E.g., leadership, teamwork, getting things done, etc.
   - **What do I do well?** Think about situations in personal or professional areas of life in which you showcased your strengths, such as collaboration, communication, or creativity.
   - **What keeps me happy?** Think about situations where you naturally flow in the task without undue anxieties, insecurities, or extreme hardship. For example, it may include mentoring, problem-solving, cross-functional collaboration, etc.
   - **How can I make the world a better place?** Think about the impact your pursued activities generate on your surrounding communities or the world at large. For example, it could be improving someone's health or well-being, making technological advancements for convenience or saving time

for others, spreading education far and wide, promoting diversity of race, conserving environmental changes, helping others improve their self-esteem, or practicing qualities of kindness, trust, love, etc.

- **What values do I hold closely?** Think about high-stake decisions and values you have exercised that have provided you with forward direction, such as honesty, humility, resilience, fairness, or integrity. Use the table *List of Values* to identify a few from *Chapter - Values for Character*.

If, for reasons, you cannot correlate and find your purpose, then you are not alone. Many find their purpose as they go along with experiences and situations in life. Until you find one, your vision could act as a purpose. While you figure out your purpose, keep pursuing things that you like or are naturally good at or enjoy doing on the side. Spending 5 percent of your off time to develop what you are good at can lead you to discover new paths over a period of time. The trick is to keep at it and keep looking until you find it. Taking things as they come and building on your interests on the side can help you formalize your purpose over a period of time.

II.   **Outline your Vision.**

Your vision is how you would like your life to be in the next 5 to 10 years horizon. Identifying this could mean challenging your ifs, buts, and only-ifs and surpassing any limiting thoughts. One way to overcome thought-centric roadblocks is to think as if you have already surpassed your challenges. They could be concerning funding, support, opportunities, resources like time, energy, etc. Ask yourself, if you didn't have these limitations, then what would your vision look like? What would you set out to achieve in your life? What would you not want to be missing 10 years from now? Your purpose and your strengths might also help contribute to developing your vision. You can expect yourself to work through the ideas and develop one statement as your vision and a couple of points to support that vision as your mission. This is your guiding path for a 10-year horizon. Initially, this could also be exercised for a shorter timeframe, for 3 to 5 years. As you get comfortable working with it, you can expand working through a longer duration of 5 to 10 years.

For instance, if you are repeatedly told you cannot reach a certain learning skill level. This could pose a good opportunity to make one of your priorities and cultivate a vision for yourself. A Vision could look like, 'I am here to take my life as a perpetual opportunity to learn and grow. Through my learning, I help others experience different forms of art and relaxation. In doing so, I set myself to take up new learning in music and arts and aim to formulate my music band in the next three years.' This exemplified a personal purpose, vision, mission, and goal alignment. The same can be extended to professional purposes, visions, missions, and goals. If the purpose converges your personal and professional endeavors, then that's the most ideal & harmonious. However, the purpose may or may not remain the same at different stages of your life across personal and professional vision.

Once you have identified your areas of focus, purpose, vision, and mission, a vision board can be created. A board which is a collage of what that reality looks like. Using pictures reflecting that reality and assembling them on a board, setting an intention to help you stay on course when reminded daily. This could be done at both levels, i.e., for personal and professional objectives.

III. **Outline your Dreams.**

Generally individuals identify or introduce themselves through their contributions, like homemakers, businesspeople, leaders, professors, etc., because they choose to spend most of their time & energy in creating life contributions in that arena. The effort that is spent to create goodwill in society. This is a direct reflection of us being creatures of creating value through building something in our individual lives. What your dreams are is a function of which area you choose to build your legacy into through your daily life contributions. Dreams for many could also include pleasure-seeking activities like achieving some position, role, title, salary, monetary valuation, etc. Expecting any outcome of your dreams is neither right nor wrong. But preferably, start with what value you'd want to create using your unique skills, abilities, and capabilities. This exercise requires you to be more outwardly focused, i.e., creating value for others rather than only gaining value from that pursuit.

Prepare a statement with 3 to 5 sentences that outline your dreams. Note that you may choose to converge your vision and dreams together or use either method in case they simplify things for you.

IV. Outline your Needs.

We have already spoken about needs and starter priorities (drivers) as part of the *Work IT Out - Master Model* & *Work IT Out - Master Model Guiding Principles* from *Chapter - The Master Model*. The following are more detailed exercises to clarify one's needs if required.

- **Priority 1: Survive**, must-haves
- **Priority 2: Sail-through**, good-to-have
- **Priority 3: Thrive**, great-to-have

Where Priority 1 is the highest priority and Priority 3 is the lowest in the order of necessity of needs.

Categorizing your needs into different priorities helps one further understand the most essential factors they need to pursue at any given time. For example, Priority 1 refers to those needs that are required to survive and are must-haves. So, Priority 2 can help one sail through their needs beyond survival, which is good-to-have. Priority 3 needs can help someone thrive once you surpass the stage of good-to-have needs and pursue those that are great-to-have in your life. Once the highest priority of survival is reasonably met, in most circumstances, one can incorporate priority good-to-have and/or great-to-have needs in their plan. Considering that the highest priorities are always met even when you are working through the next priority.

Once the needs are listed, you can make a final list of prioritized needs by asking the following questions:

1. What will your life look like if you continue to live your needs in each mode?
   - Survive
   - Sail-through
   - Thrive
2. What are the reasons why my survival needs are now required to reach thriving needs? Relate this list to your purpose and vision to identify what matters most to reach your vision.

Optionally, you may want to identify ratings for each needs category from the bold marked aspects (or just the *Building Blocks*) in the *Work IT Out - Framework*. Rate your current satisfaction for each aspect on a scale from 0 - not satisfied to 10 - very satisfied. This assessment will give you a tentative idea of what you would like to work towards and identify which ones must be included in your strategy and activity plan. Basically, you are charting a 2 by 2 decision matrix of your level of satisfaction vs. the importance of the need. Placing each need in the relevant quadrant to identify which areas would require your attention to align with your purpose & vision. An example is shown in the illustration *Needs Outlining Graph* below for three needs, e.g., work, health, and community. Scale of 0 being not satisfied to 10 being very satisfied. The bubble size here reflects the cumulative efforts assigned to that area. For example, here, *health* needs are important to pursue but reflect low satisfaction in practice while putting reasonably sufficient effort compared to *community* needs.

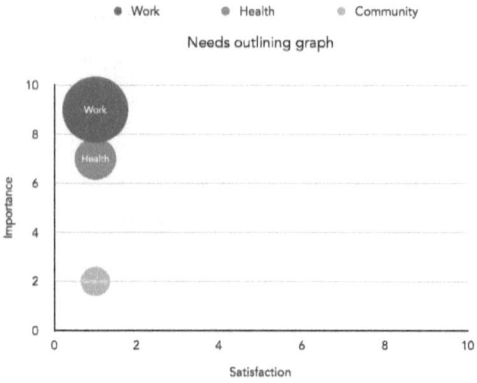

Needs Outlining Graph

V. Outline your Actions.

Having a purpose, vision/dreams, and mission is futile if no actions are charted to pursue them. Here are the steps to start your pursuit.

1. Identify which goal of the three stages supports your purpose, vision/dreams, and needs; also use *Work IT Out - Framework Chapter Guidance* mapped with *Needs*. One or more could be applicable. This helps you to prioritize your actions and their plan.
   - Living the Reality
   - Living the Dream
   - Being the Dream
2. Take a resolve to commit to this list for taking further action.
3. Identify what aspect will enable you to take action.
   - Team
   - Support
   - Sponsorship
   - Focus/attention
   - Funding
   - Prioritization

- Health
- Environment

Be specific about things you'd need to change in each category that you identified. List micro-strategies to help you remove obstacles (refer to the list you prepared from each chapter practice time exercises). Like eating healthy, following a routine of waking up and sleeping hours to manage health challenges, practicing 20 to 25 minutes sprints to focus on a given task to improve productivity & quality of output, approaching sponsors at work to support you in finding relevant opportunities, join a community to look for a team that can support you, learning to prioritize using *2 by 2 Decision Matrix for Task Prioritization*, or moving jobs or current location of work, etc. Give yourself an open runway to explore more possibilities that work for your purpose and vision.

For example, to develop a career strategy, question yourself:

- How does my current job support my purpose and vision?
- Does my current job give me a sense of achievement and engagement?
- How does my current job align with the strengths I identified in the purpose step?
- What are the criteria to realistically look for / work towards / factor in from an Industry trend standpoint?
    - Compensation
    - Career development Opportunities
    - Stability
    - Work-life balance
    - Relationships at level upwards, side-ways, downwards
    - Working hours and location flexibility
    - Recognition

VI. Bring it All Together.

Work through assembling all of it on one Strategy Board with an Action Plan. Download the *Worksheet: Work IT Out - Framework*; refer to the *Resources* section of *Chapter - Your Journey*. Once assembled, it's time to get to work. Following some tracking methods could help you stay on course and take a good view of your progress so far.

- Assigning a day, time, and hours to each micro-strategies (actions) and task. The more specific, the better.
- Tracking the progress weekly, monthly, and quarterly.
- Until the goal is reached, practice the seventh *Work IT Out - Master Model Guiding Principle - Way of Working*, discussed in *Chapter - The Master Model*.

After bringing it all together, give yourself some time to rest and recuperate. This shall bring more thoughts to refine your overall strategy. Give it a good look once again and question if any part of it needs further adjustment; please be mindful of not perfecting the plan but to look at it with an objective lens if, for now, anything needs modification before you start your journey to pursue it as the next step.

PART VII

What's Next?

*'Whatever you want to do, do it now.
There are only so many tomorrows.'*

- Michael Landon, American Actor and Filmmaker

Your Journey

> *'Luck is what happens when preparation meets opportunity.'*
>
> *- Lucius Annaeus Seneca the Younger, Stoic Philosopher of Ancient Rome*

Well done! If you have made it to this page, you have come a long way in discovering your true self and realizing your full potential. Working through this self-mentoring working guide has led you to outline an overall work-life strategy. A strategy containing your personal and professional life goals is individualized per your context, i.e., your dreams, purpose, vision, and needs. Pat yourself on the back for that!

By working through the practice time exercises and reading along each chapter, you have already showcased values of commitment, consistency, patience, perseverance, dedication, honesty, and integrity. Thank you for giving yourself this time for some inward reflections and exploring a new world within you!

All of your efforts have resulted in collective insights on key aspects of your personal & professional space, like

- That which matters in your life.
- Clarity on your defined goals.
- Prioritized goals to map your dream journey.
- Integrated goals with an overall life plan.
- Understanding oneself better through self-discovery.

- Cultivating self-knowledge and self-awareness.
- Leading activities to make change within yourself and in your surrounding environment.

> *'What doesn't kill you makes you stronger!'*
>
> *- Friedrich Nietzsche, German Philosopher*

Once practiced regularly, these would result in seamlessly integrating new behaviors. Behaviors that can help you form a positive attitude, making a positive impact in your life & environment around you. Preparing to encounter setbacks, pain, and challenges in this journey, but in the end, it'll be worth the time; it only makes you stronger as you learn from them for the future. With that approach, the next time you encounter struggles, you are flowing through them as you'll be armed with your ever-evolving wisdom. This delivers you deep meaning, satisfaction, and happiness, a true account of success!

Having said that, you may encounter some of these specific struggles.

- Internal fears, insecurities, and vulnerabilities of the unknown can keep you on the known path.
- Lacking the knowledge, resources, support, or opportunities you need on the way.
- Questioning the worthiness of pursuits & outcomes.
- Questioning your capability to achieve by harboring constant self-doubt. Or overestimating your strengths and rushing into frequent failures.
- Overwhelmed by the plan and things to do, and finding the courage to pursue micro-strategies for the first time.
- Wanting to give up upon the first or multiple accounts of failure.

Do not sweat. We've got you covered! Adopting some of the listed attitudes can ensure continuity in your pursuits.

1. Working through many things in the personal & professional arena can overwhelm anyone. Starting small and learning to work progressively can help.
2. Often, reminding yourself of your purpose or vision can help keep up the momentum.
3. Motivate yourself daily through optimistic, positive, realistic, futuristic self-talk.
4. Setbacks, struggles, and challenges are part of the journey. They give us more opportunities than create obstacles on our path. Accepting that these struggles are good for learning and growth can keep one striving for one's dreams.
5. Get consumed by improving yourself rather than getting caught up with seeking and waiting to see change in others or your surroundings. Challenging the status quo starts with being a good role model yourself. Never give up!
6. Accept that change is an incremental process of putting in bite-sized, recurring, good-quality, focused efforts, which is all you need to reach your milestones. Take one small step at a time.
7. Know what you want help with and seek help.
8. Get together as a community and lead for a cause.
9. Strive to learn how to communicate well as the situation demands.

With your curated work-life strategy, you may wonder, what's next? Where can I go from here?

1. First, ensure your *Worksheet: Work IT Out - Framework* is filled with answers to guided exercises in this book.
2. Take a printout of the plan and keep it with you. Remind yourself every day first thing in the morning to look at it. This can be done as an ongoing practice to remember what you set out to do. Additionally, review it weekly to plan your activities with a focus on what you set out to achieve during the week.
3. You can chart out the list of self-paced microlearning courses online that can aid in learning a few tangible skills in the short term

that are required to achieve your goals. And get started with that based on time allocated through the week. Likewise, list other resources like funding, team, community, learning, opportunity, and networking that will help get your goals going.

4. Track your progress through a formal Microsoft Excel worksheet (or similar software tool), mentioning task-level details. This can be updated weekly, and modifications can be made to the allocated time or schedule. Review the plan quarterly and revise it as needed.

5. Further, if you need more personalized guidance, you don't have to do it all by yourself! You can consider taking formal personal guidance based on your needs.

    a. Learning through online available microlearning courses has been a boon in today's digitally transformed world. There are skills training for everyone and every subject matter out there. All you need is good connectivity to the internet, access to the World Wide Web through a computer, and knowledge of your skill level, subject matter, time commitment, and engagement requirements about learning. You also need to explore which learning portals better serve your requirements. For example, online 101 on business communication could be a good start for basic communication skills. While for an executive level, individual needs of communication skills are different, they are more advanced & cater to a specific receiving audience of communication. Choosing the right offering for your learning stage makes learning easy, fun, appropriate, and explorative. This is a new world order; everyone's basic skill needs are met through this construct of online microlearning, regardless of whether you are an aspiring or tenured professional in the corporate world.

    b. Beyond self-learning options, mentoring can be suitably received from someone who is an expert in the field and has lived through the goals you'd like to achieve. A mentor who is open to sharing guidance with you to help you eliminate roadblocks, potentially set up formal connections, and share a different perspective or strategy with you. You will most likely need a mentor when you need a high-level approach, guidance, reviews, clarity, or direction to sort out.

c. Beyond self-learning and mentoring options, coaching can be suitably received from someone who can guide you through a strategy along with a detailed path to achieving a specific goal. Additionally, coaches can act as accountability partners and support to help you get things done. Coaches are more vested in your journey as you achieve tangible results and outcomes that keep the coach and coachee both interested in achieving the common purpose or complimenting goals. You will most likely need a coach when you know you need a high-level approach, guidance, reviews, clarity, direction, and a way to work through a specific challenge your goals impose. The type of professional coach you'd like to undertake would depend on your need, e.g., a leadership coach for developing leadership qualities, getting engaged in leadership positions, or preparing for aspirations for leadership roles. Personal growth coach for health & wellness counseling, increasing emotional intelligence, or cultivating values. Start with your required area of coaching and work backward to check on the type of coach you'd engage with.

These self-paced service options are often available as a personalized engagement based on your needs. Looking for mentors or coaches within your organization could be another way to work through seeking support. Although, there are pros and cons of doing it. While a mentor or a coach internal to the organization may easily understand work culture dynamics and your role, s/he may lack additional broader perspectives. S/he could hold biases towards organizational values, causing limits to objective guidance one can share. These individuals work best when they function in a different group or geography and report outside your immediate group or line of business. A mentor or coach external to the organization could provide a neutral outlook to achieving your goal and bring fresh new perspectives with creative ideas to adopt while broadly understanding organizational workplace dynamics. As mentioned, both have their place where they work best. Choosing an appropriate approach could positively impact your outcomes and engagement experience.

Where can one find suitable learning portals, mentors, or coaches? A good rule of thumb is finding through known referrals can be the best to engage with (after appropriate due diligence). Otherwise, as most coaches would have an online presence, searching on the internet or through professional networking websites can be worth spending time on. elementsD Coach Professional Services (eDC) is one such boutique coaching services provider. eDC helps individual professionals and corporate organizations to identify, outline, strategize, and support adequate accountability to execute their individualized personal & professional growth journey. Helping to elevate their consciousness for success the right way. Specialized mentoring & coaching offered by eDC includes the following areas.

For more details, visit www.elementsdcoach.com.

1. Workplace Culture
2. Professional Success
   a. Executive Coaching & Leadership Development
   b. Career Progression
   c. Skills Development
3. Mental Health & Well-being
   a. Mental & Emotional Wellness
   b. Behavioral Coaching
4. Holistic Lifestyle

Resources

1. Let's engage, visit www.elementsdcoach.com.
2. Share your growth journey. Write your comments or experiences to authortejalrathod@gmail.com.
3. To download the *Worksheet: Work IT Out - Framework,* visit *Resources* at www.elementsdcoach.com.
4. Gain deeper perspectives on any subjects discussed through this book by further reading from *Chapter - References.*
5. 'Listening to your self-talk for 15 minutes a day can change your life.' for scripts that can help you reprogram your beliefs set in the subconscious mind. The limited-period free mobile app can be found at https://www.selftalkplus.com/.
6. 'How do we feel' free mobile app for tracking recurring patterns of felt emotions and for taking remediation action. https://howwefeel.org/.

About Author

Author's Credentials

After spending twenty glorious years serving & bringing value to her customers in the Information Technology space, Tejal Rathod is the Founder of elementsD Coach Professional Services (eDC). She is an expert Success Coach focused on delivering coaching in areas of

- Workplace Culture
- Executive & Leadership Development
- Professional Skills
- Mental & Emotional Well-being
- Behavioral Skills
- Holistic Lifestyle for Total Health & Nutrition

Through her experience working in the corporate world, Tejal has impacted billions of dollars in customer business through digital transformations, brought convenience & happiness to millions of consumers, and trained, mentored & coached hundreds of professionals on the way. She has exercised her interest in mentoring & coaching by leading diverse teams spread over different geographies & functional roles and through various corporate & volunteering engagements.

About Author

Tejal has followed her passion for Personal Growth, Workplace Dynamics, Organization Psychology Management, and Diversity Equity Inclusion & Belonging (DEIB) related causes by pursuing relevant education, training, and experience for over ten years. Through her diverse academic pursuits in Executive Management, Psychology, and Health & Nutrition, she guides clients using a unique, holistic, integrative approach operating at a body, mind, and soul level. By which clients receive Individualized and Customized ways to achieve their Personal & Professional goals.

She caters to Individual and Corporate Organization clients through personal coaching sessions, corporate consulting engagements, curated group workshops, and community engagement. Currently, Tejal coaches worldwide professionals at the Executive level & the Early-Mid career and provides consultations to organizations. She learns by practicing the methodologies she recommends to her clients to better understand their challenges through her first-hand experiences. This makes her an empathetic coach, striving to deliver quality impact to her clients.

Tejal is also an aspiring Speaker and a Management Educator. She has a multi-faceted, dynamic personality with a passion for getting things done the right way. While not at work, she likes to keep up with her interests in arts & design, spirituality, environmental conservation, and love for the outdoors.

An Entrepreneur at heart, she has led Calibo Technologies Private Limited, her venture in business strategy and technology consulting. Additionally, her past professional experience comes from working with global technology enterprises such as Amazon Web Services, TIBCO, Tech Mahindra, et al. She has excelled in various customer-facing Technical & Management roles in Enterprise Architecture, Professional Services, Pre-Sales, and Product Management disciplines while successfully delivering business transformation goals for several Fortune 500 Enterprises, Small and Medium-scale businesses, and Start-ups across BFSI, Healthcare, & E-commerce domains, operating out of the Americas, Europe, and Asia region. She carries broad experience in architecting scalable technology solutions, leading distributed & cross-functional teams, and realizing strategic business value for global customers using technology as an enabler.

While she occasionally enjoys keeping up with the technology world, she is now focused full-time on providing professional services through coaching. Some of Tejal's highly recognized accreditations across pursued streams of expertise are:

- Corporate Strategy & Leadership, Executive Management from Indian Institute of Management - Ahmedabad (IIM-A)
  (https://www.iima.ac.in/)

- Entrepreneurship from the University of Pennsylvania (Wharton School of Business Online)
  (https://online.wharton.upenn.edu/)

- Managing Technological Innovation from Indian Institute of Management - Bangalore (IIM-B)
  (https://www.iimb.ac.in/home)

- Multiple psychotherapy modalities in the stream of Developmental, Behavioral, Cognitive, Personality, and Counseling Psychology from American Psychological Association (APA)
  (https://www.apa.org/)

- Plant-based Nutrition from T. Colin Campbell through eCornell University
  (https://ecornell.cornell.edu/)

- Ayurvedic Lifestyle Coach from The Vedic Life
  (https://thevediclife.com/)

- Meditation & Mindfulness - YACEP from Yoga Alliance
  (https://www.yogaalliance.org/)

- Bachelor of Engineering in Computer Science from University of Mumbai
  (https://mu.ac.in/)

Reach the Author

- Let's engage, visit www.elementsdcoach.com.
- Share your growth journey. Write your comments or experiences to authortejalrathod@gmail.com.

Afterword

Author's Message

I am highly enthusiastic about this first step in reaching a million professionals like you worldwide, bringing meaning & happiness to your lives. Helping you elevate yourself to *true success the right way*! I deeply believe that this journey starts with empowering you with the right information at the right time. Providing you with a plan to curate opportunities and act upon them to facilitate a change. Bringing the transformation you need to elevate the deep-seated consciousness and redirect priorities to being the dream you wish to achieve! I sincerely attempt to provide you with all the tools, techniques, knowledge and converged wisdom to highlight the guidance so that you can discover your true self & live your full potential. It's my earnest hope that this collective change, starting from within every individual professional, working through teams they are part of, and by full engagement of organizations they are working with, can help create a great working culture for the corporate world, a legacy worth leaving for the future generations.

My life so far has been about *preparation on the way* to fulfilling my purpose: to leave a legacy of bringing meaningful happiness to the lives of professionals through their personal growth. Time and again, many of my career experiences kept me in the loop of telling myself, 'Woman, work it out!'. In hindsight, I could work it out because the change started from the *self* and from *within*! Through my personal growth came about my professional success. This success idea has lasted time immemorial, and I hope this book inspires you to take charge of your success as well.

Like most of us, I had my share of struggles to manage personal and professional goals, conserve energy, and know what to do about it in a given time. Figuring everything out as I went along has made me go through a systematic phase of learning the timeless strategies that work. Through the rush of responsibilities, I often needed an easy-to-follow individualized approach, which is captured through this self-help working guide. Here, I have assembled the learnings that I have applied myself and that have seen great results. Techniques & aspects that are ever relevant & useful, and knowledge that can be accessed by anyone. Through these levers, I am reaching out to professionals functioning in any role so that the corporate world sees the wave of positive change in work culture through the collective outcomes of their endeavors.

Throughout my career, I have encountered numerous professionals, just like me, who were disappointed to see three main obstacles in their path to success, i.e., the obstacle of not knowing, of not taking a leap of faith to change, and of succumbing to the realities as they are choosing not to evolve. I could find the knowledge & guidance I sought from different individuals through books and working in different types of organizations, customer businesses & roles. Solutions were all scattered amongst different times, places, and circumstances across my professional journey. This book gives me an opportunity to serve the needs of those seeking similar guidance to achieve their dreams, whether personal or professional. Culminating the most essential & time-tested direction in one place, easily available at the right time and for the right consumption. So that everyone can have access to more opportunities leading to the effective achievement of their life dreams.

Through my endeavors, I eventually found all that I indeed sought, incrementally making progress toward challenging goals. Every single time, I took an opportunity to learn from those difficulties. Through this book, I hope opportunities find you much before you seek them out. An opportunity to be in a position to save your health, a true wealth of life. An opportunity to integrate your personal & professional life holistically and sustainably. An opportunity to create an impact in the world through your success. An opportunity to bring meaning and happiness. For that very reason, through this book, I intend to make a deep impact in your life through your efforts, using the guidance applicable specifically to you.

As I take my next step in being part of your journey to achieve your

Afterword

dreams via your growth, this book is a stepping stone to empower you with a beginner's tool, capturing advanced drivers of success. In the hope and intention that you will find your mentor or coach within yourself. This will help you discover your true self and evolve the whole community of professionals together, one step at a time. My mission to positively contribute to the growth journey of a million of you starts here by passing on the knowledge I have been fortunate to receive from divinity, legacy, and my life experiences. Through this knowledge, I hope you *Empower* yourself, inspire you to *Transform* yourself, and elevate your consciousness to *Evolve* yourself.

Change is formidable but possible when you take a leap of faith and allow yourself a chance. A chance to *Empower* is good, *to Transform* is better, but to *Evolve* is the best!

Take a step forward; start your journey now. Never give up!

With Love & Light.

Acknowledgments

This book reserves its acknowledgments to my Gurus in life. My heartiest obeisances to the Supreme Personality of Godhead, Lord Krishna, the cause of all causes, who appeared in ~3200 BCE. I express my earnest gratitude for his eternal grace and mercy, which arranged all the experiences and people in my life the way they did. I thought, '..because they stayed true to their ways, I chose to evolve.'. But the truth was, it was the hand of a higher power at play to make me be, reach, and carry on my current path. '..because of his grace, I chose to evolve for the better!'. Thank you for bringing knowledge, blessings, love, connection, and belonging into my life. Thank you for helping me stay focused through the intention & works of this book.

With the highest reverence, I express my gratitude to His Divine Grace Abhay Charanaravinda Bhaktivedanta Swami Prabhupāda, Founder-Acharya of the International Society of Krishna Consciousness, for being the Guru I needed. His teachings have inspired me to gain higher perspectives and a direction in life. His grit & simplicity have inspired me to live a life of dignity. His numerous contributions to spiritual literature have inspired me to write. A. C. Bhaktivedanta is widely regarded as the modern era's foremost Vedic scholar, translator, and teacher. He is respected as the world's most prominent contemporary authority on bhakti-yoga. At age sixty-nine, he became the first-ever translator and commentator on over eighty volumes of the Vedas' most important sacred bhakti texts, including the Bhagavad-gītā and Śrīmad-Bhāgavatam. He introduced 'India's message of peace and goodwill' to the Western world, inspiring thousands of Westerners & Indians and launching one of the fastest-growing spiritual movements in the history of the world. Beyond his immense contributions, his unmatched endeavors in uniting humanity by the motto of *Simple Living High Thinking* have motivated me to live a meaningful life. I thank all of his disciples who crossed my path for sharing inspirational guidance and being friendly well-wishers.

I also like to thank my ancestors for giving me capabilities that I can cultivate further and continue their lineage through my endeavors, my grandparents from the Rathod & Chauhan families for being role models & providing a healthy environment while growing up, my parents for their care & support, and my spouse for his companionship.

This book would not have been possible if it were not for those numerous authors who reached me through their knowledge & experiences in the form of non-fiction books. I would also like to thank all the qualified doctors, mentors, and coaches who came on my path through their work in the modern & ancient fields of medicine and psychology. Their research and years of experience have helped evolve my understanding and depth of knowledge about the healthcare space. It would not be possible to name them all. Still, I am grateful to each one of them for having learned from, especially from the authors and medical professionals who have significantly impacted my life.

My thanks to the India Authors Academy for sharing the publishing process, making it possible for this book to reach all of you.

And finally, many thanks to all of you who chose to spend your valuable time reading and working through what I had to offer you for your personal & professional growth. As it takes only a few words to resonate and motivate anyone, I hope that this book empowers you with the required knowledge, inspires you to transform yourself, and elevates you to evolve your consciousness in whichever minuscule way or form possible. It's a privilege to be part of your journey; thank you for allowing me to be there with you.

References

PART II. Living the Reality!

1. The Art of Motivation Maintenance, Why some givers burn out but others are on fire. Give & Take by Adam Grant (2013), Pg 182.
2. Start with Why, how great leaders inspire action at TEDxPugetSound. By Simon Sinek (2009) https://youtu.be/u4ZoJKF_VuA.
3. Rumbling with Leadership, Armed leadership weaponing Fear and Uncertainty. Dare to Lead by Brene Brown (2018), Pg 104.
4. Overcoming laziness. By Scott Heferrey (2024) https://scottjeffrey.com/how-to-overcome-laziness/.
5. 25 Things about life I wish I had known 10 years ago. By Darius Foroux (2024). https://dariusforoux.com/25-things-about-life/.
6. Growth Mindset concept. Mindset: The New Psychology of Success by Carol Dweck (2006).
7. Individual & Organizational Mindset at Future of Work Conference - Wharton School. Carol Dweck & Angela Duckworth (2022) https://youtu.be/gDeUMy-IMmE?feature=shared.
8. Teaching a Growth Mindset at Stanford. By Carol Dweck (2015) https://youtu.be/isHM1rEd3GE?feature=shared.
9. Letters to disciple Krishna Das. Difference between animal and human being is that an animal has no intelligence and therefore is not expected to follow any regulative principles, but human life is a life of responsibility. By A.C. Bhaktivedanta Swami (1970) https://vaniquotes.org/wiki/Difference_between_animal_and_human_being_is_that_an_animal_has_no_intelligence_and_therefore_is_not_expected_to_follow_any_regulative_principles,_but_human_life_is_a_life_of_responsibility.
10. Sundar Pichai: 'Reward efforts, not outcome' on Leadership & Management at Stanford Business School of Graduate (2022) https://www.gsb.stanford.edu/insights/sundar-pichai-reward-effort-not-outcomes.
11. How to Enhance Performance & Learning by Applying a Growth Mindset at Huberman Lab Podcast By Andrew Huberman (2023) https://youtu.be/aQDOU3hPci0?feature=shared.
12. Daring Leadership, Cultivating Commitment and Shared Purpose. Dare to Lead by Brene Brown (2018), Pg 100.
13. Apple's Directly Responsible Individual - DRI model (2023) https://handbook.gitlab.com/handbook/people-group/directly-responsible-individuals/.
14. What is a RACI Matrix? At Project Management Principles. By Lauren Good (2023-2024) https://project-management.com/understanding-responsibility-assignment-matrix-raci-matrix/.

References

15. The Basics of Self-Trust, Braving Trust. Dare to Lead by Brene Brown (2018), Pg 233-234.
16. How Shame Shows up at Work, Rumbling with Vulnerability. Dare to Lead by Brene Brown (2018), Pg 131.

PART III. Living the Dream!

17. Organize the company around the people whose impact is the highest, Culture - Believe Your Own Slogans. How Google Works by Eric Schmidt & Jonathan Rosenberg (2014-2017), Pg 47.
18. 2 by 2 decision matrix - Eisenhower Decision Matrix by Dwight D. Eisenhower https://en.wikipedia.org/wiki/Time_management#The_Eisenhower_Method.
19. How Learning Actually Happens in Making More Mistakes. Creatures of Discomfort. Hidden Potential by Adam Grant (2023), Pg 41.
20. Nonviolent Communication, NVC at The Center for Nonviolent Communication. By Dr. Marshall Rosenberg (1985-2024) https://www.cnvc.org/, https://en.wikipedia.org/wiki/Nonviolent_Communication.
21. Start with Why, how great leaders inspire action at TEDxPugetSound. By Simon Sinek (2009) https://youtu.be/u4ZoJKF_VuA.
22. Towards a holistic understanding of human motivation: core values—the entrance to people's commitment?. AI & SOCIETY, 17, 150-180. Dahlgaard, S. M. P., & Dahlgaard, J. J. (2003) https://link.springer.com/article/10.1007/s00146-003-0257-y.
23. Decision making, 21 Timeless Principles for Life from Ramayana by Dr. Shubha Vilas (2024).
24. Armed leadership, The armory - Rumbling with Leadership. Dare to Lead by Brene Brown (2018), Pg 104.
25. List of Values, Living into our Values. Dare to Lead by Brene Brown (2018), Pg 188.
26. Invisible Leadership. Open-Eyed Meditations by Dr. Shubha Vilas (2016) Pg 182, 221.
27. Ways of Creating Value to Maximize Your Life. By 7Mindsets https://7mindsets.com/creating-value/.
28. How Google Works Summary | PDF, Chapters & Review of Erik Schmidt & Jonathan Rosenberg's Book : MunchWeb https://munchweb.com/how-google-works-summary-pdf-chapters-review-of-eric-schmidt-jonathan-rosenberg-book.
29. Five Attitudes That Are Important in Workplaces in Small Business, Managing Employees,Types of Employees - CHRON. By Lynda Moultry Belcher (2019) https://smallbusiness.chron.com/five-attitudes-important-workplaces-19114.html.
30. 25 Things about life I wish I had known 10 years ago. By Darius Foroux (2024) https://dariusforoux.com/25-things-about-life/.
31. The Art of Motivation Maintenance, Why some givers burn out but others are on fire. Give & Take by Adam Grant (2013), Pg 182.
32. How to Recognize the Real Culprit: Your Internal Critic. The Teacher's Ultimate Stress Mastery Guide: 77 Proven Prescriptions to Build Your Resilience, 35. Helmstetter, S. (2012) https://books.google.co.in/books?hl=en&lr=&id=jABECgAAQBAJ&oi=fnd&pg=PA35&dq=shad+helmstetter+belief+model&ots=m_YmjxuHkJ&sig=fxjrZljG7b9GGeb_iIm UrpA5fd8.
33. We Learn to Believe, The Wall, Passing It On, The Self Management Sequence, The Motivation Myth. What to Say When You Talk To Yourself by Shad Helmstetter, Ph.D. (1982-2016).

References

34. Shifting Perspectives, It's Not (Always) Your Fault. What Works for Women at Work by Joan C. Williams & Rachel Dempsey (2014-2018), Pg 10.
35. Implementing diversity, equity, inclusion, and belonging management in organizational change initiatives. IGI Global. El-Amin, A. (Ed.). (2022) https://books.google.co.in/books?id=V2V2EAAAQBAJ&printsec=frontcover&source=gbs_ge_summary_r&cad=0#v=onepage&q&f=false.
36. The list of masculine and feminine traits is taken from the Bern Sex Role Inventory, the standard test used for accessing perceptions of gender roles in The Double Mind, Spotting Tightrope Patterns. What Works for Women at Work by Joan C. Williams & Rachel Dempsey (2014-2018), Pg 63.

PART IV. Being the Dream!

37. Book reference: Emotional Intelligence by Daniel Goleman (1995).
38. What Emotional Intelligence Looks Like: Understanding The Four Skills. Emotional Intelligence 2.0 by Travis Bradberry & Jean Greaves (2009) Pg. 24.
39. Characteristics of emotional maturity and emotional immaturity. Evidence-Based S4E1: Disentangling from Emotionally Immature People with Lindsay C. Gibson, PsyD (2023) https://youtu.be/ysr6qF1szfI?feature=shared.
40. Chapter 18 Text 63, Conclusion - The Perfection of Renunciation. Bhagavad-gītā As It Is by His Divine Grace A.C. Bhaktivedanta Swami Prabhupāda (1972-1986), Pg 893. Or https://vedabase.io/en/library/bg/18/63/.
41. Bhakti Yoga: the Yoga of Devotion at Yoga Basics. By Timothy Burgin (2023) https://www.yogabasics.com/learn/bhakti-yoga-the-yoga-of-devotion/.
42. Saranagati, Bhagavad-gītā by Dr. Shubha Vilas (2024). https://www.youtube.com/playlist?list=PLgVlBJa-Cj5UMJVJvWOnrpmWFN8Tk_j9k
43. Maslow's Hierarchy of Needs, paper "A Theory of Human Motivation" in the journal Psychological Review. By Maslow, Abraham H. (1943).
44. Illustration reprinted from Maslow's Hierarchy of Needs in Psychology at Simply Psychology. By Saul Mcleod, PhD (2024) https://www.simplypsychology.org/maslow.html and https://en.wikipedia.org/wiki/Maslow%27s_hierarchy_of_needs.
45. How to Apply Maslow's Hierarchy of Needs to Your Business in BusinessManagement, MillionaireMentor. By Moe Nawaz (2023) https://www.linkedin.com/pulse/how-apply-maslows-hierarchy-needs-your-business-moe-nawaz.
46. Pichère, P., & Cadiat, A.-C. (2015). *Maslow's hierarchy of needs*. Lemaitre.
47. What is the Experience of Integrating Your Shadow Like? The Shadow by Scott Jeffery (2024) https://scottjeffrey.com/wp-content/uploads/Shadow-Work-Guide.pdf.
48. 25 Things about life I wish I had known 10 years ago. By Darius Foroux (2024) https://dariusforoux.com/25-things-about-life/.
49. The China Study by T. Colin Campbell Center for Nutrition Studies (2020) https://nutritionstudies.org/the-china-study/.

PART VI. THE Plan!

50. PERMA-V Framework in Highlights from Experts Series. At Davidson Institute (2020). Authored by Nuntiya Smith CAPP, APPC https://www.davidsongifted.org/gifted-

blog/perma v framework/.
51. Finding Your Purpose, 21 Timeless Principles for Life from Ramayana by Dr. Shubha Vilas (2024).
52. Workplace health promotion, employee wellbeing and loyalty during COVID-19 Pandemic—Large scale empirical evidence from Hungary. Economies, 9(2), 55. Gorgenyi-Hegyes, E., Nathan, R. J., & Fekete-Farkas, M. (2021) https://www.mdpi.com/2227-7099/9/2/55.
53. Applying the PERMA model in employee wellbeing. e-mentor. Czasopismo naukowe Szkoły Głównej Handlowej w Warszawie, 99(2), 39-46. Wilczyński, A., & Kołoszycz, E. (2023) https://bibliotekanauki.pl/articles/2231194.pdf.
54. Seven questions can clarify what really matters to you.Use Strategic Thinking to Create the Life You Want, The Big Idea Series / Strategize Your Life in Personal Purpose and Values. By Rainer Strack, Susanne Dyrchs, and Allison Bailey (2023) https://hbr.org/2023/12/use-strategic-thinking-to-create-the-life-you-want.
55. Defining Culture, History & Society. Written by Leslie A. White (2022) https://www.britannica.com/topic/culture.
56. Bursting Career Myths: The Path to True Professional Growth in CareerManagement. By Adity Mohanty (2023) https://www.linkedin.com/pulse/bursting-career-myths-path-true-professional-growth-adity-mohanty.
57. Vision Board. The Secret by Rhonda Byrne's (2006).
58. Agile Methodology Sprint (2006) https://en.wikipedia.org/wiki/Scrum_(software_development).
59. Physiology and interpersonal relationships. The Cambridge handbook of personal relationships, 385-405. Loving, T. J., Heffner, K. L., & Kiecolt-Glaser, J. K. (2006) http://ndl.ethernet.edu.et/bitstream/123456789/65494/1/29.pdf.pdf#page=408.
60. Would Longevity Make Us Happier? The Role of Social Relations in the Link between Happiness and Aging. Journal of Aging & Social Change, 13(1). Nozaki, Y. (2023) https://search.ebscohost.com/login.aspx?direct=true&profile=ehost&scope=site&authtype=crawler&jrnl=25765310&AN=169956374&h=koZ8cqSMX4oWuS9iByT50CYTyHPLFZmA0QL9%2FJKSA3zs%2BUibPlBbV0a%2Fo6dhtfRnf08JdWp0lHSTKErIMwxPTg%3D%3D&crl=c.

PART VII. What's Next?

61. 'How do we feel' free mobile app for tracking recurring patterns of felt emotions and for taking remediation action. By Ben Silbermann, co-founder of Pinterest & his team along-with Dr. Marc Brackett & his team at the Yale University Center for Emotional Intelligence (2020) https://howwefeel.org/.
62. Timelines of Hindu texts. Wikipedia, the free encyclopedia (2010-2023) https://en.wikipedia.org/wiki/Timeline_of_Hindu_texts.
63. Krishna. Wikipedia, the free encyclopedia (2002-2024) https://en.wikipedia.org/wiki/Krishna.
64. A. C. Bhaktivedanta Swami Prabhupāda. Wikipedia, the free encyclopedia (2002-2024) https://en.wikipedia.org/wiki/A._C._Bhaktivedanta_Swami_Prabhupada.
65. Dialectic Spiritualism - A Vedic View of Western Philosophy https://dialecticspiritualism.com/.
66. About Us – Bhaktiyoga Live https://bhaktiyoga.live/about-us/.

References

67. Srila Prabhupada | Palace of Gold https://www.palaceofgold.com/srila-prabhupada.

www.ingramcontent.com/pod-product-compliance
Lightning Source LLC
Chambersburg PA
CBHW031614210526
45464CB00004B/1567